the new york times

100 GREAT COUNTRY SONGS

edited by Richard Broderick

Quadrangle/The New York Times Book Co.

To Steve Sholes—
Country Music Hall of Fame member
and my friend—thanks.

About the songs in this book

To include everybody's choices for the
Top 100 Country Hits would suddenly
change the book to the Top 1,000
Country Hits. The reasons for exclusion
vary: a few permissions were received
after the book went to press, several
songs extended to seven or more pages
and would not fit...but included is
a cross-section of country songs—most
of which topped the country charts
at some time in their history.

First printing, November, 1973.

Library of Congress Catalog Card Number: 73-79907
International Standard Book Number: 0-8129-0376-5

Photos courtesy of: Country Music Foundation

Music Typography: **Music Art Co.**
Music Proofreading: **Frank Metis**
Jacket and Interior Design: **Jerry Lieberman**

CONTENTS

A SATISFIED MIND

Words and music by Red Hays and Jack Rhodes

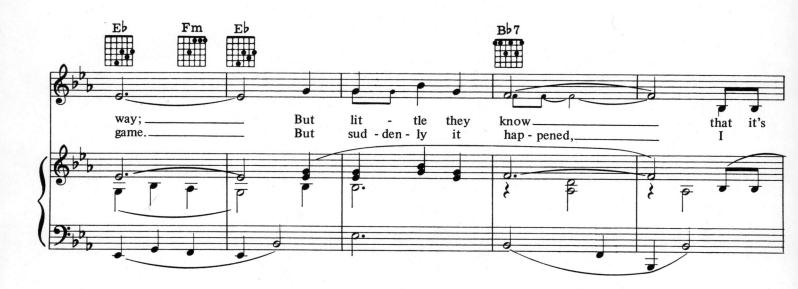

way; _____ But lit - tle they know _____ that it's
game. _____ But sud - den - ly it hap - pened, _____ I

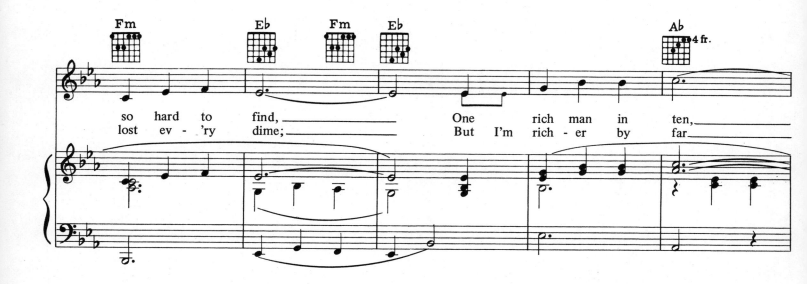

so hard to find, _____ One rich man in ten, _____
lost ev - 'ry dime; _____ But I'm rich - er by far _____

_____ With A Sat - is - fied Mind. _____ 2.Once I was
_____ With A Sat - is - fied

Mind. _____

3. Mon - ey can't   buy   back   your
4.(When life has) end - ed,   my

youth when you're old, _____   Or a friend when you're lone - ly _____
time has run out, _____   My friends and my loved ones _____

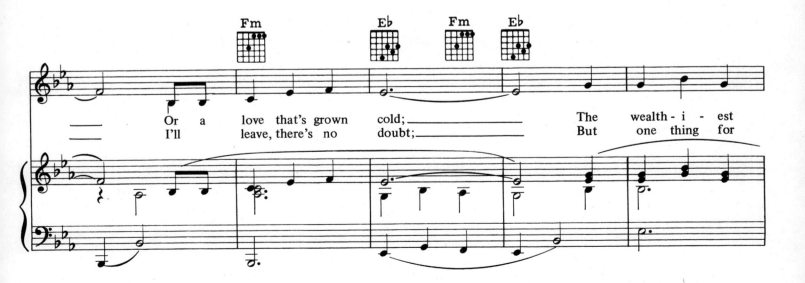

_____ Or a love that's grown cold; _____   The wealth - i - est
I'll leave, there's no doubt; _____   But one thing for

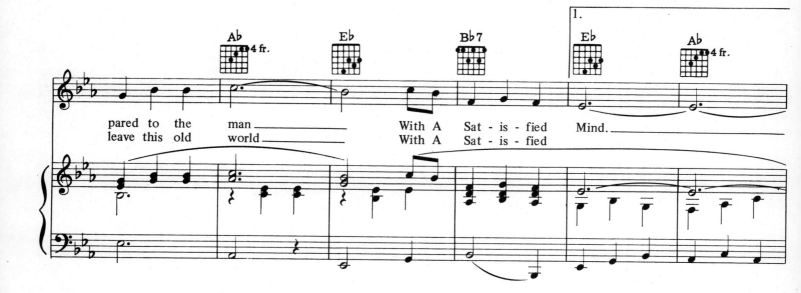

A WORRIED MAN

Words and music by Dave Guard and Tom Glazer

Moderato

It takes A Wor-ried Man To sing a wor-ried song; It takes A Wor-ried Man To sing a wor-ried song; It

takes A Wor-ried Man To sing a wor-ried song. I'm wor-ried

now,_____ But I won't be wor-ried long._____

Fine

1. ___ Got my-self a Cad-il-lac, Thir-ty dol-lars down;
2. ___ I've been a-way on a bus-'ness trip, Trav-'lin' all a-round.___
3. Well, Bob-by's in the liv-ing room Hold-ing hands with Sue,___

Got my-self a brand new house_ Five miles out of town;___
I've got a gal and her name is Sue,___ Pret-ti-est gal in town.___
Nick-ie's at that big front door, 'Bout to come on thru.___ She
Well,

AM I THAT EASY TO FORGET?

Words and music by Carl Belew and W. S. Stevenson

Moderately, with a beat

They say you've found some-bod-y new, But that won't stop my lov-in' you, I just can't let you walk a-way,

For-get the love I had for you.   Guess I could find some-bod - y

too,   But I don't want no one but you,

How could you leave with - out re - gret?   Am I That Eas - y To For-

get?   Be - fore you leave,   be   sure you find

You want ‹ her / his › love   much more than mine,   'Cause I'll just say we've

nev - er met,   If I'm that eas - y to for - get.

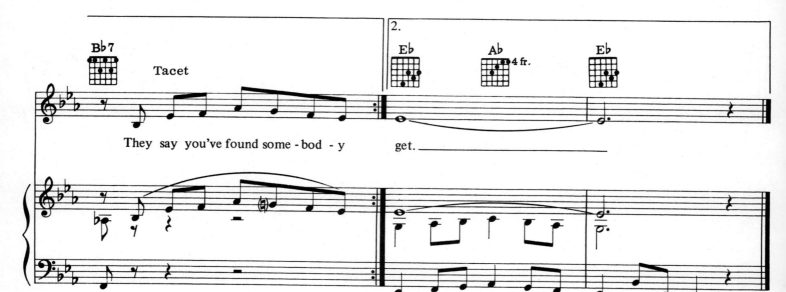

Tacet

They say you've found some - bod - y   get. _____

ANY TIME

Words and music by Herbert Happy Lawson

Time _____ you feel down-heart-ed, _____ That will

prove _____ your love for me is true. _____ An - y

Time _____ you're think-ing 'bout me, _____ That's the time _____

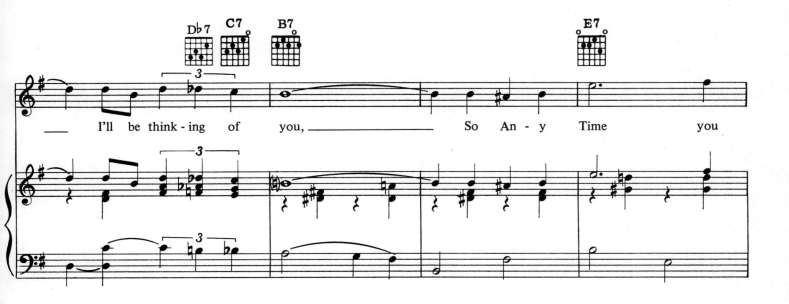

I'll be think - ing of you, _____ So An - y Time you

say you want me back a - gain, That's the time I'll

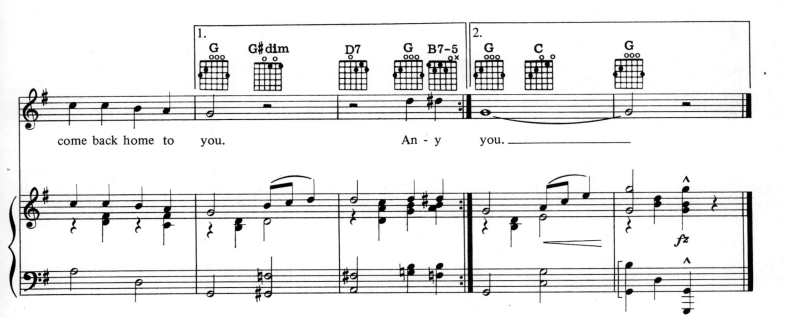

come back home to you. An - y you. _____

ANY WAY YOU WANT ME

Words and music by Aaron Schroeder and Cliff Owens

Chorus:

I'll___ be as strong___ as a moun-tain___ or weak___ as a wil-low tree.___ An - y Way You Want Me,___ well, that's___ how I will

be._____ I'll___ be as tame as a ba-by____ or

wild___ as the rag-ing sea._____ An-y Way You

Want Me,_____ well, that's_ how I will be._____ In your hands_ my

heart is clay, to take and mold___ as you may._____

BACK IN THE SADDLE AGAIN

Words and music by Gene Autry and Ray Whitley

Moderately

I'm Back In The Sad - dle A - gain,

Out where a friend is a friend, Where the

long horn cat - tle feed, on the low - ly jim - son weed; I'm

Back In The Sad - dle A - gain. _____

Rid - in' the range once more, _____

Tot - in' my old for - ty - four, _____ Where you

sleep out ev - 'ry night, where the on - ly law is right; I'm

Back In The Sad - dle A - gain.

Whoo - pi - ti - yi - yo, Rock - in' to and fro,

BILLY BAYOU

Words and music by Roger Miller

Moderately

Verse:

1. Back a-bout eigh-teen hun-dred and some, A
2. Bil-ly was a boy kind of big for his size,

Louis-i-an-a cou-ple had a red-head-ed son.
Red hair and freck-les and big blue eyes.

No name fit - ted him — Jim, Jack or Joe,
Thir - teen years from the day he was born,

They just called him Bil - ly Ba - you.
Bil - ly fought the bat - tle of Lit - tle Big Horn.

Chorus:
Bil - ly, Bil - ly Ba - you, watch where you go! You're walk - ing on quick - sand,

Additional Verses:

3. One sad day Billy cried ho, ho,
   I can whip the feathers off Geronimo.
   He smarted off and the chief got mad,
   That like to have ended our Louisiana lad. *(To Chorus)*

4. One day in eighteen seventy-eight
   A pretty girl walked thru Billy's front gate.
   He didn't know whether to cry out or run,
   And now he's married 'cause he did neither one. *(To Chorus)*

BLUE SUEDE SHOES

Words and music by Carl Lee Perkins

Bright tempo (not too fast)

Chorus:

Well, it's one for the mon-ey, two for the show, three to get read-y, now

go, cat, go! But don't you step on my Blue Suede

BORN TO LOSE

Words and music by Ted Daffan

Moderately

Born To Lose, I've lived my life in vain; _____ Ev-'ry
(Born To) Lose, my ev-'ry hope is gone; _____ It's so

dream has on-ly brought me pain; _____ All my
hard to face that emp-ty dawn; _____ You were

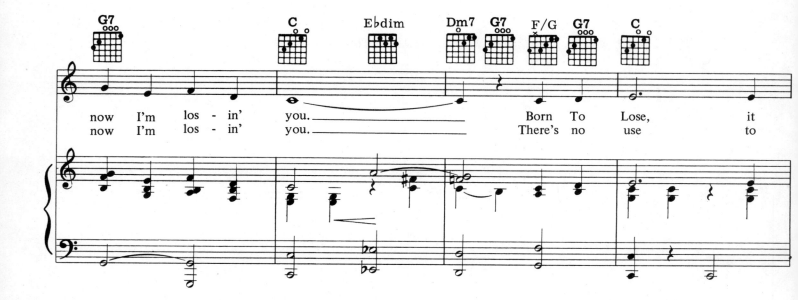

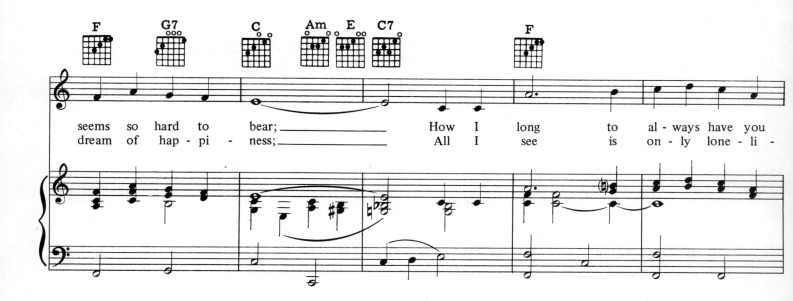

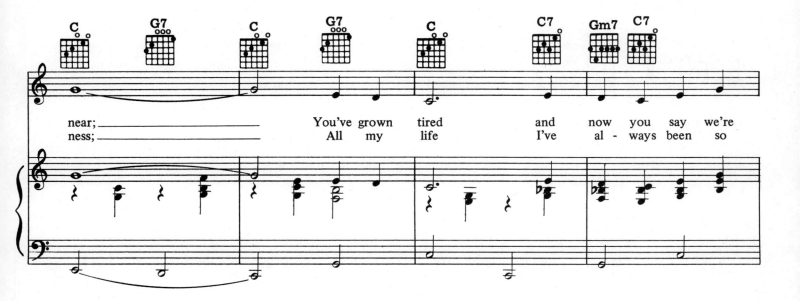

near;_____ You've grown tired and now you say we're
ness;_____ All my life I've al - ways been so

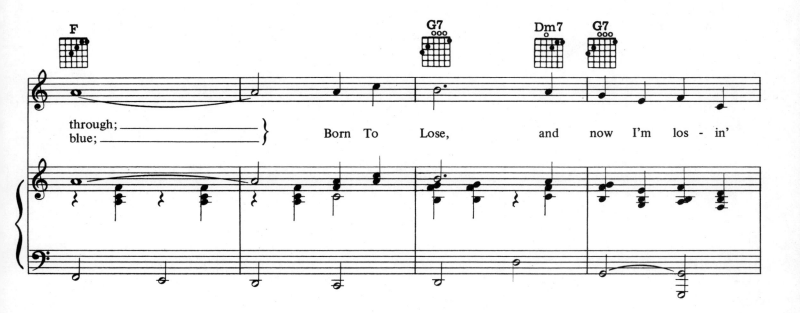

through;_____ } Born To Lose, and now I'm los - in'
blue;_____ }

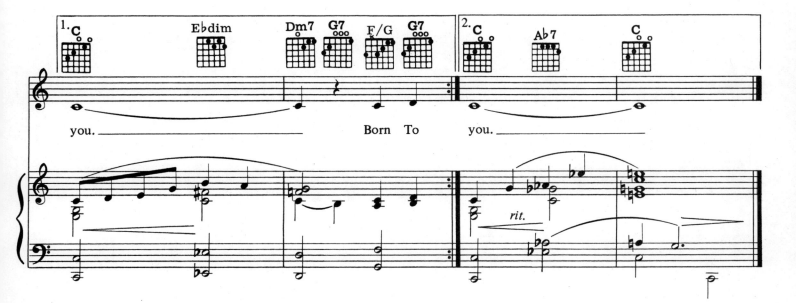

1. you._____ Born To 2. you._____

rit.

BOUQUET OF ROSES

Words and music by Steve Nelson and Bob Hilliard

Moderately, not too fast

1. I'm send - ing you a big Bou - quet Of Ros - es, ____
2. (You) made our lov - er's lane a road of sor - row, ____

____ One for ev - 'ry time you broke my heart, ____
Till at last we had to say good - bye. ____

And   as   the   door   of   love   be - tween   us   clos - es,
You're   leav - ing   me   to   face   each   new   to - mor - row,

Tears   will   fall   like   pet - als   when   we   part.
With   a   bro - ken   heart   you   taught   to   cry.

I   begged   you   to   be   diff - 'rent   but   you'll
I   know   that   I   should   hate   you   af - ter

al - ways   be   un - true,   I'm   tir - ed   of   for -
all   you've   put   me   thru',   But   how   can   I   be

giv - ing,   Now there's noth - ing left to do.
bit - ter,   When I'm still in love with you?   1.-2. So I'm

send - ing you a big Bou - quet Of Ros - es, _____

_____ One for ev - 'ry time you broke my

heart. _____   2. You   heart. _____

BURNING BRIDGES

Words and music by Walter Scott

Verse:

1. Found some let-ters you wrote me this morn-ing,_____ They
2. (So the) love_____ we once planned to-geth-er,_____ Said good-

told of the love we once knew,_____ Now they're
bye to the friends we once knew,_____ Then I

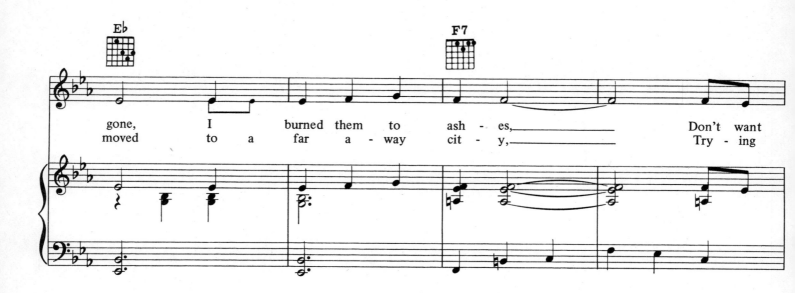

gone, I burned them to ash - es,_____ Don't want
moved to a far a - way cit - y,_____ Try - ing

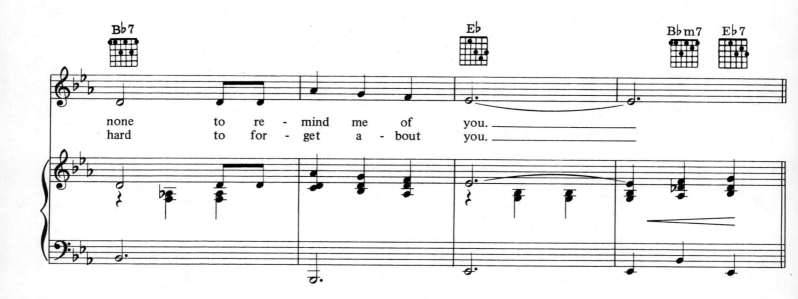

none to re - mind me of you._____
hard to for - get a - bout you._____

Chorus:

Burn - ing Bridg - es be - hind me,_____ It's too

CANDY KISSES

Words and music by George Morgan

1. Can - dy Kiss - es_____ wrapped in pa - per_____
   cas - tle_____ out of dreams, dear,_____

_____ mean more to you_____ than an - y of
_____ I thought that you_____ were build - ing one

love words_____ in my ear._____
sad - ness,_____ on - ly tears._____ } Can - dy

Kiss - es_____ wrapped in pa - per_____

_____ mean more to you_____ than mine do,

dear._____ 2. I built a dear._____

CHANTILLY LACE

Words and music by J. P. Richardson

Moderate boogie woogie

(Ha - ha - ha - ha - ha)   *(Spoken)*   Oh, you sweet thing!

Do   I   what?   Will   I   what?

Oh, Baby,   you   know   what   I   like!

Refrain:

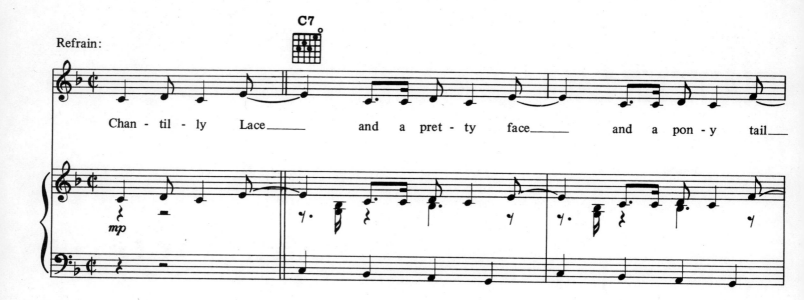

Chan - til - ly Lace____ and a pret - ty face____ and a pon - y tail__

— hang - in' down,___ Wig - gle in her walk and a gig - gle in her

talk, Makes the world go 'round,_____ Ain't

noth-in' in this world like a big eyed girl___ to make me act so fun-ny, make me

spend my mon-ey, make me feel real loose like a long-necked goose, like a

girl. *(Spoken)* (Oh, Baby, that's-a what I like.)   girl. *(Spoken)* (Oh, Baby, that's-a what I like.)

CIGAREETES, WHUSKY AND WILD, WILD WOMEN

Words and music by Tim Spencer

Verse:

1. Once I was hap-py and had a good wife, I had e-nough mon-ey to last me for life, I
2. Now I am fee-ble and bro-ken with age, The lines on my face make a well writ-ten page, I'm
3. Write on the cross at the head of my grave, "For wom-en and whus-ky here lies a poor slave," Take

met with a gal, and we went on a spree, She
leav - ing this sto - ry, how sad but how true, On
warn - ing, dear strang - er, how take warn - ing, dear friend, Then

taught me to smoke____ and drink____ whus - ky;
wom - en to and whus - ky and what they will do;
write in big let - ters these words at the end;

Chorus:

Cig - a - reetes and whus - ky and wild, wild

wom - en, They'll drive you cra - zy, They'll drive you in -

CINDY, OH CINDY

Words and music by Bob Barron and Burt Long

Segue to Verse Fine

let - ter soon___ And I'll be home - ward

G   Em   C   G   Fine

bound. ___

Verse:

G   Em   C

1. I joined the na - vy to see the world,___ But no - where could I
2. I see her face___ in ev - 'ry wave,___ Her lips kiss ev - 'ry
3. I know my Cin - dy's wait - ing, As I walk the deck a -

mp

find   A girl as sweet___ as Cin - dy,___ The
breeze,   Her lov - in' arms___ reach out for me, Through
lone,   Her lov - in' arms___ reach out for me, Soon

girl I left be - hind.___ I've sailed the wide___ world o -
calm and storm - y seas.___ At night I pace___ the lone -
I'll be head - in' home.___ Then my sail - in' days will be o -

D.S.
(after 3rd Verse al Fine) 𝄋

- ver,_____ Can't get her out of my mind._____
- ly deck, Ca - ressed by mem - o - ries._____
- ver_____ And no more will___ I roam._____

COOL WATER

Words and music by Bob Nolan

throats burnt dry and souls that cry for wa - ter
wake and yawn and and souls car - ry on to wa - ter
hear our pray'r and show us where there's wa - ter
like to rest where there's no quest for wa - ter

wa - ter wa-ter wa-ter wa - ter

Cool, clear wa - ter.
Cool, clear wa - ter.
Cool, clear wa - ter.
Cool, clear wa - ter.

Chorus: wa - ter wa - ter wa - ter

Keep a-mov-in', Dan, don't you lis-ten to him, Dan, He's a dev-il, not a man, and he

CRYING IN THE CHAPEL

Words and music by Artie Glenn

Slowly, with expression

Chorus:

1. You saw me Cry - ing In The Chap - el, _____ The tears I shed were tears of
2. (Ev - 'ry sin - ner looks for some - thing _____ That will put his heart at

joy; _____ I knew the mean - ing of con - tent - ment, _____
ease; _____ There is on - ly one true an - swer, _____

DANG ME!

Words and music by Roger Miller

Verse:
(Spoken)

1. Well,   here   I   sit high   gettin'   ideas,   Ain't   nothin' but a   fool   would
2. Just   sittin' round drinkin' with the   rest   of the guys, ____   six rounds bought   and
3. They say   roses   are   red   and   violets   are purple, ____   sugar's sweet and   so is

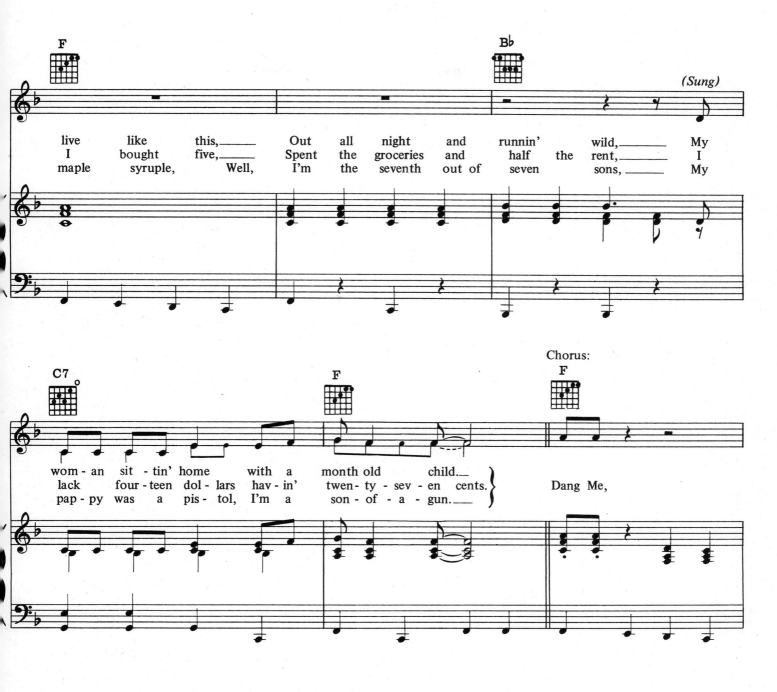

high from the high - est tree, Wom - an, would you weep for

me!

DEEP IN THE HEART OF TEXAS

Words by June Hershey Music by Don Swander

un - der - stand, And it's there I long to be. _____

Refrain:

*Clap, Clap, Clap,

The stars at night are big and bright,
The cov - otes night wail a - long the trail,

Clap.

Deep In The Heart Of Tex - as; _____ The prair - ie
Deep In The Heart Of Tex - as; _____ The rab - bits

Clap, Clap, Clap, Clap.

sky is wide and high, Deep In The Heart Of
rush a - round the high brush, Deep In The Heart Of

* (Clap hands.)

64

DETOUR

Words and music by Paul Westmoreland

1. Head-ed down life's crook-ed road, lot of things I nev-er knowed, And
2. (When I) got right to the place where if said "A-bout Face," I
3. (When I) got stuck in the mud, all my hopes dropped with a thud, I

cause of me not know-in' I now pine. Trou-ble
thought that all my wor-ries were be-hind. But the
guess that my heart strings are made of twine. Had no

got in the trail spent the next five years in jail,_____ Should have
far - ther I go the more sor - row I_____ know,_____ Should have
will pow - er to get from the hole that I'm in yet,_____ Should have

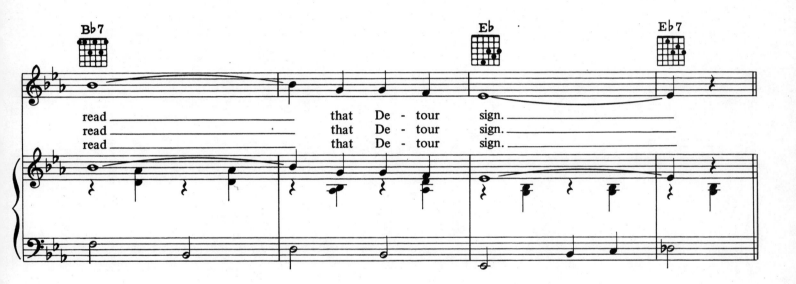

read _____ that De - tour sign. _____
read _____ that De - tour sign. _____
read _____ that De - tour sign. _____

Chorus:

De - tour,_____ There's a mud - dy road a -

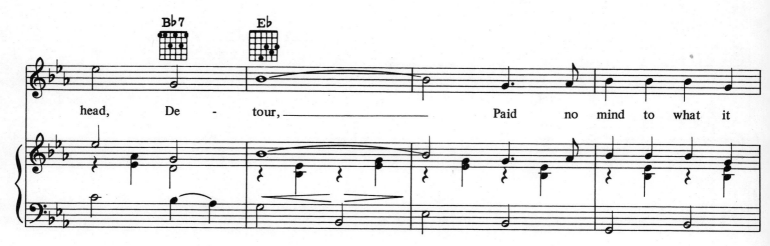

head, De - tour, _____ Paid no mind to what it

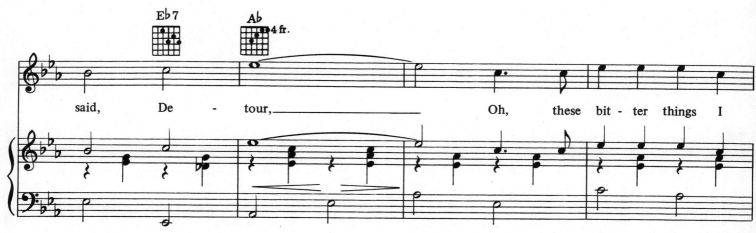

said, De - tour, _____ Oh, these bit - ter things I

find, should have read _____ that De - tour

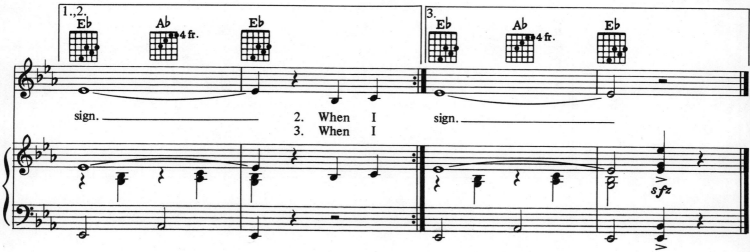

sign. _____ 2. When I sign. _____
3. When I

DEVIL WOMAN

Words and music by Marty Robbins

Mar - y took me back a - gain, _____ She said if I want - ed my

free - dom I could be free ev - er - more, _____ But

I don't want to be and I don't want to see Mar - y cry an - y-

Chorus:

more. Dev - il Wom - an, _____ Dev - il Wom - an, let

2. Mary is waiting and weeping alone in our shack by the sea,
   Even after I hurt her, Mary's still in love with me,
   Devil Woman, it's over, trapped no more by your charms,
   I don't want to stay, I want to get away, woman, let go of my arms.

3. Devil Woman, you're evil like the dark coral reef,
   Like the winds that bring high tides, you bring sorrow and grief,
   You made me ashamed to face Mary, barely had the strength to tell,
   Skies are not so black, Mary took me back, Mary has broken your spell.

4. Running alone by the seashore, running as fast as I can.
   Even the sea gulls are happy, glad I'm coming home again,
   Never again will I ever cause another tear to fall.
   Down the beach I see what belongs to me, the one I want most of all.

Last Chorus

Devil Woman, Devil Woman, don't follow me,
Devil Woman, let me be, just leave me alone, I want to go home.

DON'T TAKE YOUR GUNS TO TOWN

Words and music by Johnny Cash

Moderately

Chorus:

1. A young cow-boy named Bil - ly Joe grew rest - less on the farm. A
2. He laughed and kissed his mom and said: "Your Bil - ly Joe's a man.

boy filled with wan - der - lust, who real - ly meant no harm. He changed his clothes and
I can shoot as quick and straight as an - y - bod - y can. But I would - n't shoot with -

shined his boots and combed his dark hair down, And his moth-er cried as he walked out: }"Don't
out a cause; I'd gun no-bod-y down." But she cried a-gain as he rode a-way;

Take Your Guns To Town, son; Leave your guns at home, Bill; Don't

Take Your Guns To Town." 2. He Town."

3. He sang a song as on he rode, his guns hung at his hips.
   He rode into a cattle town, a smile upon his lips.
   He stopped and walked into a bar and laid his money down,
   But his mother's words echoed again: "Don't Take Your Guns To Town, son;
   Leave your guns at home, Bill; Don't Take Your Guns To Town."

4. He drank his first strong liquor then to calm his shaking hand,
   And tried to tell himself at last he had become a man.
   A dusty cowpoke at his side began to laugh him down.
   And he heard again his mother's words: "Don't Take Your Guns To Town, son;
   Leave your guns at home, Bill; Don't Take Your Guns To Town."

5. Bill was raged and Billy Joe reached for his gun to draw.
   But the stranger drew his gun and fired before he even saw.
   As Billy Joe fell to the floor the crowd all gathered 'round
   And wondered at his final words: "Don't Take Your Guns To Town, son;
   Leave your guns at home, Bill; Don't Take Your Guns To Town."

Engelbert Humperdinck

Johnny Cash

Kris Kristofferson

Tom T. Hall

WWVA Jamboree, Wheeling, W. Va.

DON'T TAKE YOUR LOVE FROM ME

Words and music by Henry Nemo

Verse:
You could take my cas - tle, that's if I had a cas - tle, and I'd
You could take my trea - sure, that's if I had a trea - sure, and I'd

miss it for just a while,

face pov - er - ty with a smile,

But there's one thing I ask of you, one thing you must nev - er do. Tear a

life is yours to make, so please keep the spark a - wake. Would you

just a sigh?_____ All this your heart won't let you do,_____ This is what I

beg of you, Don't Take Your Love From Me._____

EASY LOVING

Words and music by Freddie Hart

Eas - y Lov-ing, so sex-y look-ing,

I know from the feel-ing that it comes from the heart.

Eas - y Lov-ing, ev-'ry days Thanks-

giv - ing,_____ to count all my bless - ings I would-n't know_where to

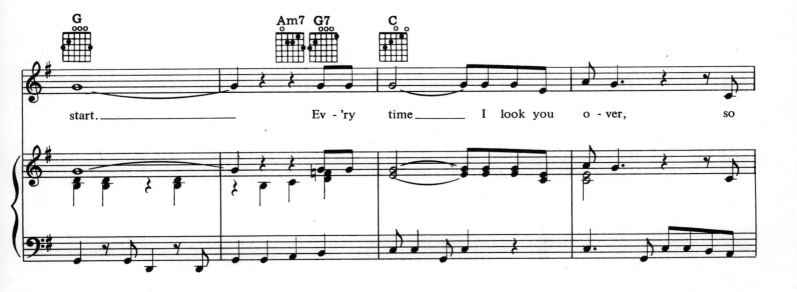

start._____ Ev - 'ry time_____ I look you o - ver, so

real to life it seems. Up - on your_ pret - ty shoul - ders there's a

pair of   an - gel wings._____   Eas - y Lov-ing,_____

see - ing's be - liev - ing,_____   Life___ with you's like   liv - ing

in a beau-ti-ful dream.   dream._____

80

EL PASO

Words and music by Marty Robbins

Moderato

Out in the West Tex - as town of El Pa - so, I fell in
Night - time would find me in Ro - sa's can - ti - na, Mu - sic would

love with a Mex - i - can girl. _____
play and Fe - li - na would whirl. _____

I was in love but in vain I could tell. _____
I had but one chance and that was to run. _____
My love is strong-er than my fear of death. _____
I have to make it to Ro-sa's back door. _____

One night a wild young cow-boy came in, Wild as the
Out through the back door of Ro-sa's I ran, Out where the
I sad-dled up and a-way I did go, Rid-ing a-
Some-thing is dread-ful-ly wrong, for I feel a deep burn-ing

West Tex-as wind. _____
hors-es were tied. _____
lone in the dark. _____
pain in my side. _____

Dash - ing and dar - ing, a drink he was shar - ing with wick - ed Fe -
I caught a good one, it looked like it could run, Up on its
May - be to - mor - row a bul - let will find me, To - night noth - ing's
Though I am try - ing to stay in the sad - dle, I'm get - ting

li - na, the girl that I loved. _____ So in an - ger, I
back and a - way I did ride _____ Just as fast as I
worse than this pain in my heart. _____ And at last, here I
wear - y, un - a - ble to ride. _____ But my love for Fe -

chal - lenged his right for the love of this maid - en, Down went his hand for the
could from the West Tex - as town of El Pa - so, Out to the bad - lands of
am on the hill o - ver - look - ing El Pa - so, I can see Ro - sa's can -
li - na is strong and I rise where I've fall - en, Though I am wear - y I

84

85

EVERYBODY'S TALKIN'

Words and music by Fred Neil

stop-pin', star-in', I can't see the fac-es, On-ly the

shad-ows _____ of their eyes. _____

I'm ___ go-in' where the sun ___ keeps shin-in' thru the pour-in' ___ rain,

Go-in' where the weath-er ___ suits my clothes. _____

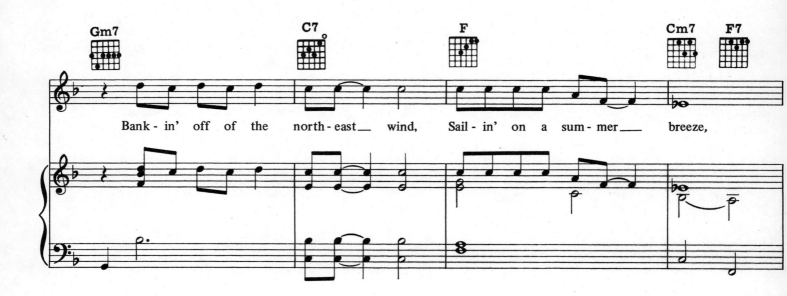

Bank-in' off of the north-east___ wind, Sail-in' on a sum-mer___ breeze,

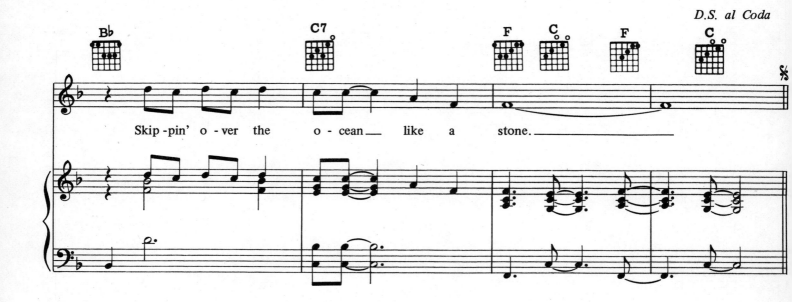

Skip-pin' o-ver the o-cean___ like a stone.___

D.S. al Coda

Repeat and fade

Coda

___ And
I won't___ let you leave my love___ be-hind. _____ No,
I won't___ let you leave my love___ be-hind. _____ And,
I won't___ let you leave my love___ be-hind. _____

FADED LOVE

Words and music by John Wills and Bob Wills

1. As I look at the let - ters that you wrote to me, It's
2. (I ___) think of the past and all the pleas - ures we had, As I

you that I'm think - ing of, ___ As I
watch the mat - ing of the dove, ___ It was

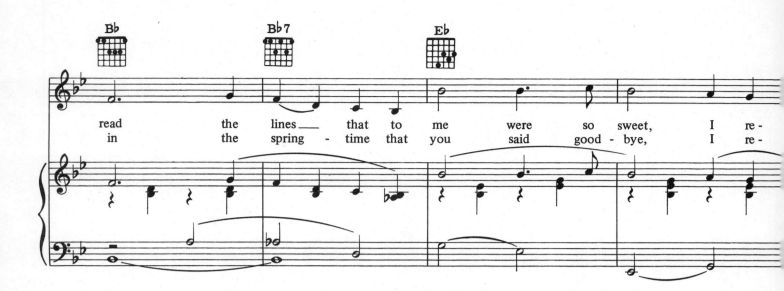

read   the   lines ___ that to me   were so sweet,   I re -
in   the   spring - time that you   said good - bye,   I re -

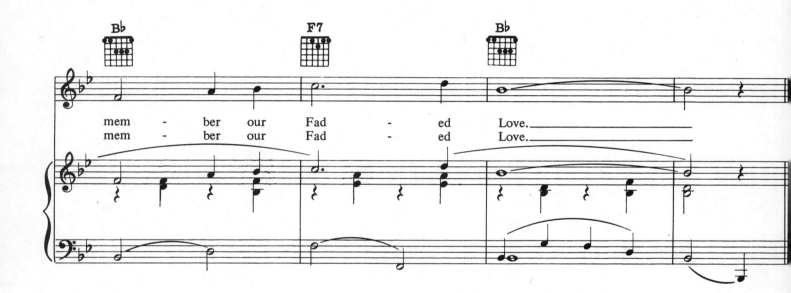

mem - ber   our Fad   -   ed   Love. ___
mem - ber   our Fad   -   ed   Love. ___

Chorus:

I miss   you, dar - ling, more and more ev - 'ry

day,   As heav - en   would   miss   the   stars   a - bove. _____

With   ev -   'ry   heart - beat   I   still

think   of   you,   And   re - mem - ber   our   Fad - ed

Love.   2. I _____   Love. _____

FOLSOM PRISON BLUES

Words and music by Johnny Cash

3. I bet there's rich folks eatin' in a fancy dining car.
   They're prob'ly drinkin' coffee and smokin' big cigars,
   But I know I had it comin', I know I can't be free,
   But those people keep a-movin', and that's what tortures me.

4. Well, if they freed me from this prison, if that railroad train was mine.
   I bet I'd move it over a little farther down the line,
   Far from Folsom Prison, that's where I want to stay,
   And I'd let that lonesome whistle blow my blues away.

FROM A JACK TO A KING

Words and music by Ned Miller

From A Jack To A King,_____ From lone-li-ness to a wed-ding ring,

I played an ace and I won a queen,_____ And walked a-way with your

heart. From A Jack To A King,

With no re-gret I stacked the cards last night, And la-dy luck played her

hand just right To make me king of your heart.

For just a lit-tle while, I thought that I might

lose the game. Then just in time, I saw the twin-kle in your

eye._____ From A Jack To A King,_____ From lone-li-ness to a

wed-ding ring, I played an ace and I won a queen, You made me queen of your

heart. From A Jack To A heart._____

GALVESTON

Words and music by Jimmy Webb

glow - ing, ___ She was twen - ty - one. ___ When I left Gal - ves - ton.
flash - in'. ___ I clean my gun. ___ And dream of Gal - ves - ton.

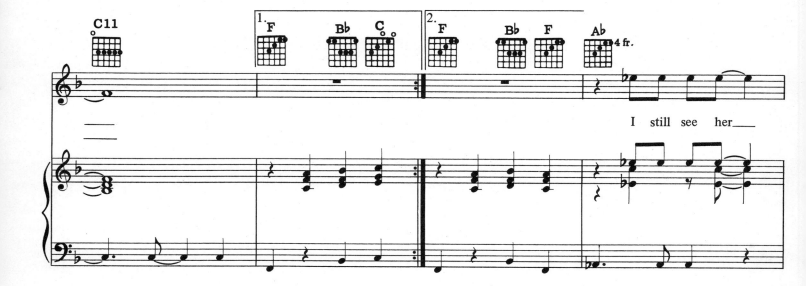

___ I still see her ___

stand - ing by ___ the wa - ter; ___ Stand - ing there,

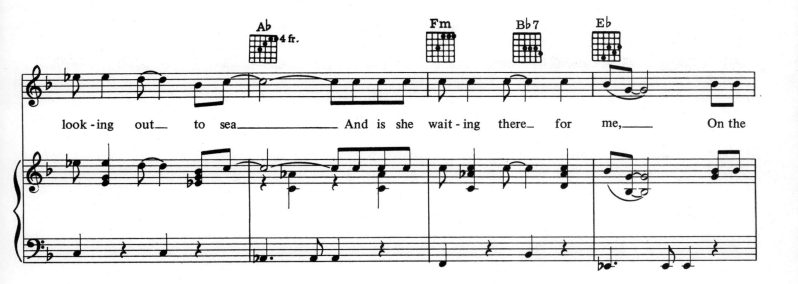

look-ing out__ to sea_____ And is she wait-ing there__ for me,__ On the

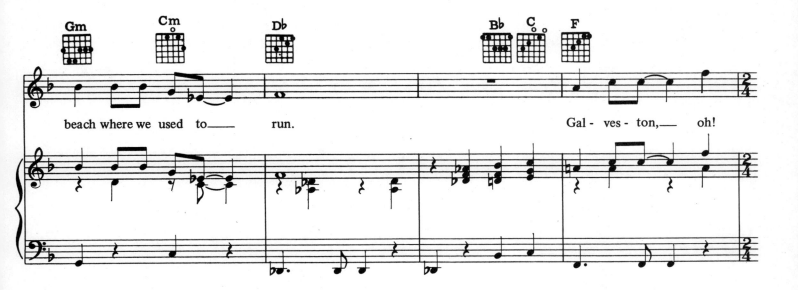

beach where we used to__ run. Gal - ves - ton,__ oh!

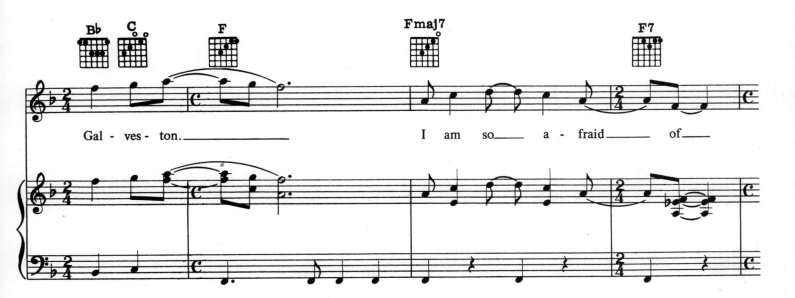

Gal - ves - ton._____ I am so a - fraid__ of__

dy - ing.___ Be - fore I dry___ the tears she's cry - ing.___

Be - fore I watch___ your sea birds fly - ing in___ the sun___

at Gal - ves - ton, ___ at Gal - ves - ton.___

GENTLE ON MY MIND

Words and music by John Hartford

Moderately bright

C   Cmaj7   C6   Cmaj7

1. It's know-ing that your door is al - ways o - pen and your path is free to
2. (It's not) cling-ing to the rocks and i - vy plant-ed on their col - umns now that binds
3. (Though the) wheat fields and the clothes lines and junk - yards and the high - ways come be-tween
4. (I) dip my cup of soup back from the gur-glin' crack - lin' caldron in some train

Dm

walk,   That
me   Or
us   And
yard   My

Dm7

That keeps you in the back-roads by the
That you're mov-ing on the back-roads by the
But not to where I can-not see you walk -
That you're wav-ing from the back-roads by the

Dm6　　　Dm7　　　　　　Dm　A+5　Dm7　　　G7

riv - ers of my mem'ry that keeps you ev - er Gen - tle On My
riv - ers of my mem'ry and for hours you're just Gen - tle On My
in' on the back - roads by the riv - ers flow - ing Gen - tle On My
riv - ers of my mem'ry ev - er smil - in' ev - er Gen - tle On My

1.2.3.
C

Mind.　　　　　　　　　　　　　　　　　　　　　It's

4. C

Mind.

103

GUESS THINGS HAPPEN THAT WAY

Words and music by Jack Clement

Moderately

Chorus:

1. You ask me if I'll for - get my ba - by. I guess I will some day.
2. You ask me if I'll miss her kiss - es. I guess I will ev - 'ry day.

I don't like it, but I Guess Things Hap - pen That

Way.

You ask me if I'll get a - long.___
You ask me if I'll find an - oth-er.

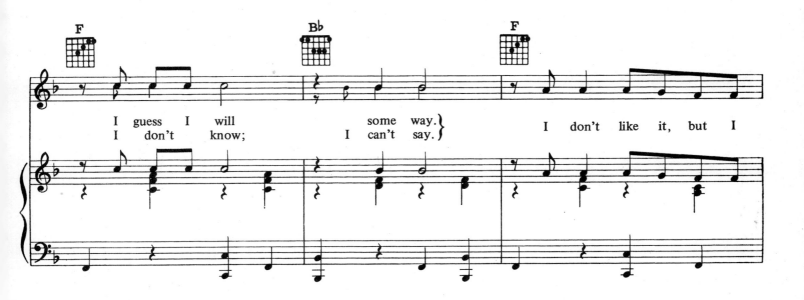

I guess I will   some way.
I don't I know;   I can't say.

I don't like it, but I

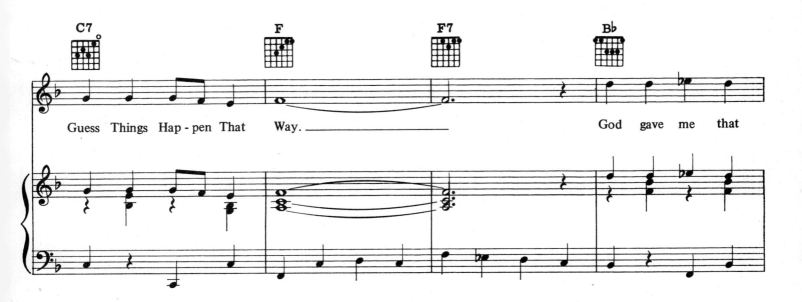

Guess Things Hap - pen That Way.___

God gave me that

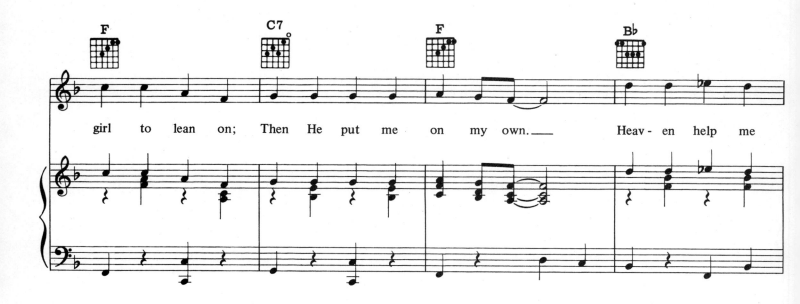

girl to lean on; Then He put me on my own.___ Heav-en help me

be a man and have the strength to stand a-lone.___ I don't like it, but I

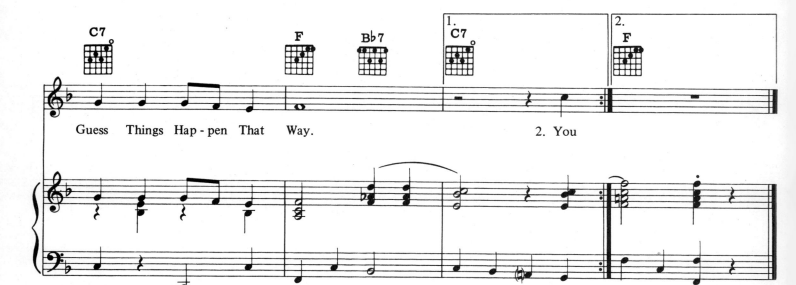

Guess Things Hap-pen That Way. 2. You

HEARTACHES BY THE NUMBER

Words and music by Harlan Howard

Moderato

Verse:

Bb   Eb

1. Heart - ache Num - ber One was when you left me,_____ I
2. Heart - ache Num - ber Three was when you called me,_____ And

F7   Bb

nev - er knew that I could hurt this way._____ And
said that you were com - ing back to stay._____ With

more.   Yes, I've got Heart-aches By The Num - ber,____ A

love that I can't win,   But the day   that I stop count - ing,   That's the

day my world will   end. _____   day my

world   will   end. _____

HEARTBREAK HOTEL

Words and music by Mae Boren Axton, Tommy Durden and Elvis Presley

1. Since my ba - by left me, found a new place to
4. If your ba - by leaves you and you have a tale to

dwell. Down at the end of Lone - ly
tell, Just take a walk down Lone - ly

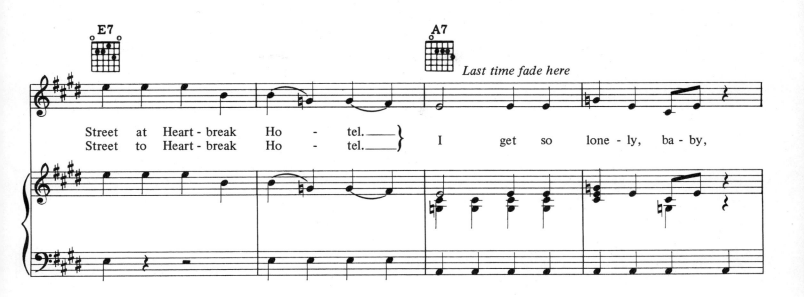

Street at Heart-break Ho - tel. _____ } I get so lone - ly, ba - by,
Street to Heart-break Ho - tel. _____

Last time fade here

I get so lone - ly. I get so lone - ly I could

die. 2. Al -

2. though it's al - ways crowd - ed, still can find___ some room,
3. Bell - hop's tears keep flow - ing, desk clerks dressed__ in black.

where those bro - ken heart - ed lov - ers cry a - way their gloom, oh!
They been so long on Lone - ly Street they ain't nev - er gonn' come back, oh!

I get so lone - ly, I get so lone - ly

After 2nd time
D.S. Lyric 4 and fade

get so lone - ly I could die.

HE'LL HAVE TO GO

Words and music by Joe Allison and Audrey Allison

Put your sweet lips a lit-tle clos-er to the phone,
Whis-per to me, tell me do you love me true,

Let's pre-tend that we're to-geth - er, all a - lone.
Or is he hold-ing you the way I do?

say the words I want to hear, while you're with an-oth-er man, If you

want me, an-swer "Yes" or "No", Dar-ling, I will un-der-stand. Put your

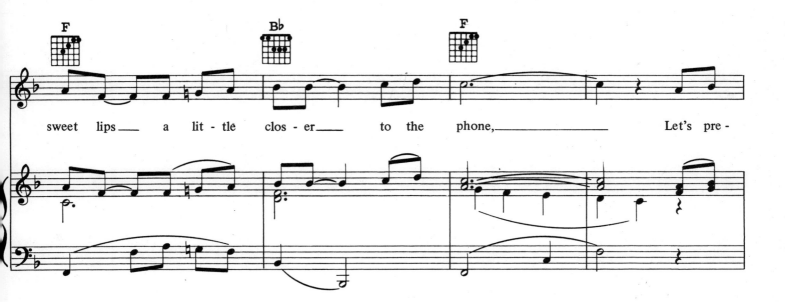

sweet lips___ a lit-tle clos-er___ to the phone,_____ Let's pre-

tend that we're to - geth - er, all a - lone,_____ I'll tell the

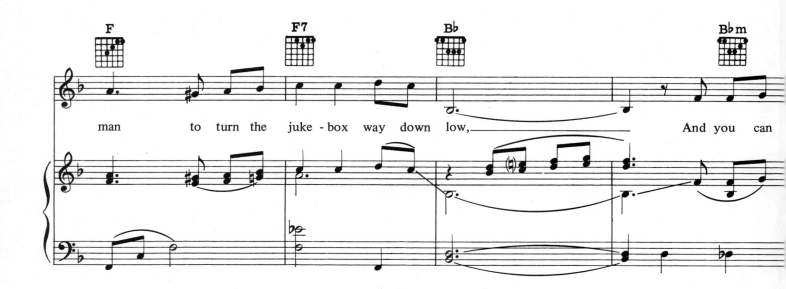

man to turn the juke - box way down low,_____ And you can

tell your friend, there with you,___ He'll Have To Go._____

poco a poco ritard.

HELLO WALLS

Words and music by Willie Nelson

1. Hel - lo, Walls, How'd things go for you to - day? Don't you
(2. Hel - lo,) win - dow, Well, I see that you're still here. Aren't you

miss her since she up and walked a - way? And I'll
lone - ly since our dar - lin' dis - ap - peared? Well, look

bet you dread to spend an-oth-er lone-ly night with me, But,
here, is that a tear-drop in the cor-ner of your pane, Now,

lone-ly walls, I'll keep you com-pa-ny._____ 2. Hel-lo,
don't you try to tell me that it's

rain._____ She went a-way and left us all a-lone

the way she planned. Guess we'll have to learn to get a-long with-

out her if we can. Hel-lo, ceil-ing,___ I'm gon-na stare at you a-

while, You know I can't sleep, so won't you bear with me a-

while? We must all pull to-geth-er or else I'll lose my

mind, 'Cause I've got a feel-in' she'll be gone a long, long time.___

HELP ME MAKE IT THROUGH THE NIGHT

Words and music by Kris Kristofferson

1. Take the rib - bon from your hair,
2. Come and lay down by my side,
Yes - ter - day is dead and gone,

Shake it loose and let it fall,
Till the ear - ly morn - in' light,
And to - mor - row's out of sight,

Lay - in' soft up - on my skin,_____
All I'm tak - in' is your time._____
And it's sad to be a - lone._____ *(To Fine)*

1.

Like the shad - ows on the wall.

2.

To next strain

Help Me Make It Thru The Night.

Fine

Help Me Make It Thru The Night. _____

I don't care who's right or wrong,

I don't try to un-der-stand.

Let the dev-il take to-mor-row.

D.S. al Fine 𝄋

Lord, to-night I need a friend.

HIGH NOON

Words by Ned Washington Music by Dimitri Tiomkin

Moderato

Do not for - sake me, oh my dar - lin,'_____

On this our wed - ding day._____

And I must face a man who hates me, _____

Or lie a cow - ard,   A cra - ven cow - ard,

Or lie a cow - ard in my grave! _____

_____ Oh, to be torn 'twixt love and du - ty, 'spos-in' I lose my

fair - haired beau - ty, Look at that big hand move a - long____ near - in' High

Noon. He made a vow while in state's pris - on, Vowed it would be my

life or his - 'n, I'm not a - fraid of death but, oh,____ what will I

do if you leave me? Do not for -

sake me, oh my dar - lin', _____ You made that

Eb7   Ab   C7   Fm

prom - ise as a bride. _____ Do not for -

Ebdim   Eb   Eb7   Ab

sake me, oh my dar - lin', _____ Al - tho' you're

Eb   Ab   Eb   Ab

griev - in', don't think of leav - in', Now that I

HONEYCOMB

Words and music by Bob Merrill

Moderato

Chorus: Hon-ey-comb, won't-cha be my ba-by? Hon-ey-comb, be my own. Just a hank of hair and a piece of bone, made a walk-in' talk-in' Hon-ey-comb.

Made a Hon - ey - comb.___ Then they combed the world and they
Next they made a bird.___ Now they wait - ed 'round till the
So they called it love.___ Then they went a - round look - in'

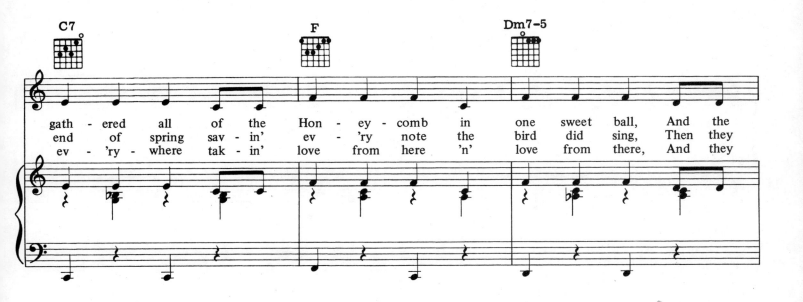

gath - ered all of the Hon - ey - comb in one sweet ball, And the
end of spring sav - in' ev - 'ry note the one bird did sing, And Then they
ev - 'ry - where tak - in' love from here 'n' love from there, And they

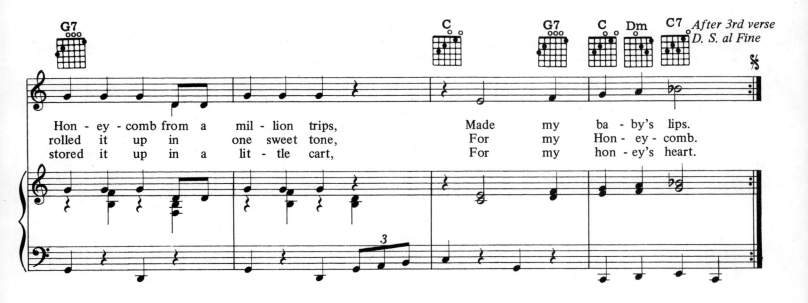

Hon - ey - comb from a mil - lion trips, Made my ba - by's lips.
rolled it up in one sweet tone, For my Hon - ey - comb.
stored it up in a lit - tle cart, For my hon - ey's heart.

After 3rd verse
D. S. al Fine

HOUND DOG

Words and music by Jerry Leiber and Mike Stoller

Medium Bright Rock

ff

Chorus:
Tacet

ff

You ain't noth-in' but a Hound Dog, _____ cry-in' all the time.

You ain't noth-in' but a Hound Dog, _____

cry - in' all the time.

Well,___ you ain't

nev - er caught a rab - bit and you ain't no friend__ of mine.

Tacet

When they said you was high - classed,

well, that was just a

lie.

When they said you was high - classed,

well, that was just a lie. Well, ___ you ain't

nev - er caught a rab - bit and you ain't no friend ___ of mine.

You ain't noth - in' but a ___ mine. ___

[HOW MUCH IS] THAT DOGGIE IN THE WINDOW

Words and music by Bob Merrill

much is That Dog - gie In The Win - dow?_____ I (Bark! Bark!)

do hope that dog - gie's for sale. _____ 1. I 2. I

must take a trip____ to Cal - i - for - nia _____ And
read in the pa - pers there are rob - bers _____ With

leave my poor sweet - heart a - lone, _____ If
flash - lights that shine in the dark; _____ My

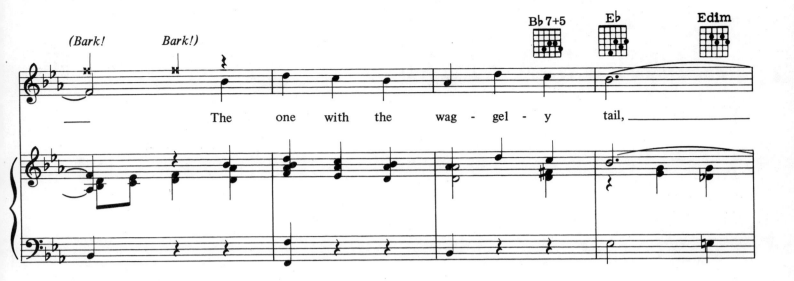

(Bark! Bark!)

The one with the wag - gel - y tail, _____

How much is That Dog - gie In The Win - dow, _____

(Bark! Bark!)

I do hope that dog - gie's for sale. _____

I ALMOST LOST MY MIND

Words and music by Ivory Joe Hunter

baby,   I Al - most Lost My Mind. _____ My
peo - ple,   I can't tell who I meet. _____ 'Cause
gyp - sy,   And had my for - tune read. _____ I
peo - ple,   The news was not so good. _____ She

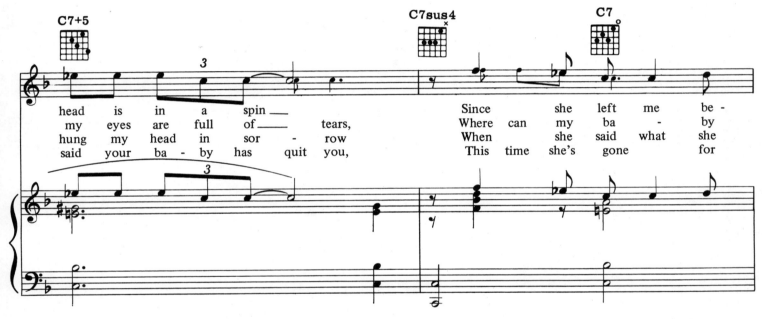

head is in a spin _____ tears,   Since she left me be - by
my eyes are full of _____ tears,   Where can my ba - by be?
hung my head in sor - row   When she said what she said.
said your ba - by has quit you,   This time she's gone for good.

hind. _____
be? _____
said. _____
good. _____

1.2.3.

2. I
3. I
4. Well,

4.

I DON'T HURT ANYMORE

Words by Jack Rollins Music by Don Robertson

out of my mind,___ I can't be-lieve that it's true!___ I've for-got-ten some-how___

that I cared so be-fore.___

___ And it's won-der-ful now;___ I Don't Hurt An-y-more.

Tacet
I Don't Hurt An-y-more.___

I FALL TO PIECES

Words and music by Harlan Howard and Hank Cochran

want me to for-get, pre-tend we've nev-er met; ____
one who'll love me, too, the way you used to do; ____

And I've tried ____ and I've tried, but I
But each time ____ I go out with ____

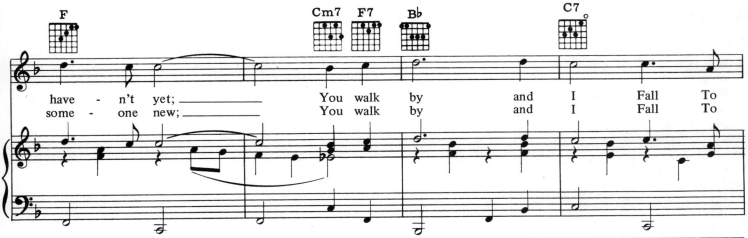

have -n't yet; ____ You walk by and I Fall To
some - one new; ____ You walk by and I Fall To

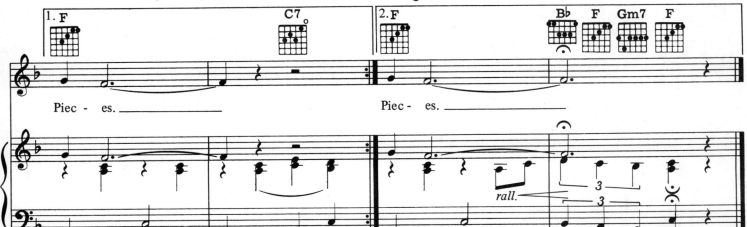

1. F C7
Piec - es. ____

2. F ..... Bb F Gm7 F
Piec - es. ____
rall.

I'M MOVIN' ON

Words and music by "Hank" Snow

On, _____ I'll soon be gone, _____ You were
on, _____ Oh, hear my song. _____ You had
on, _____ Keep roll - in' on. _____ You're gon -
On, _____ I'm roll - in' on. _____ You have
on, _____ You stayed a - way too long. _____ I'm _____

fly - in' too high for my lit - tle old sky, _____ so I'm Mov - in'
the laugh on me, so I've set you free, _____ and I'm Mov - in'
na ease my mind, so put me there on time, _____ keep roll - in'
bro - ken your vow and it's all o - ver now, _____ so I'm Mov - in'
through with you, too bad you are blue, _____ so keep mov - in'

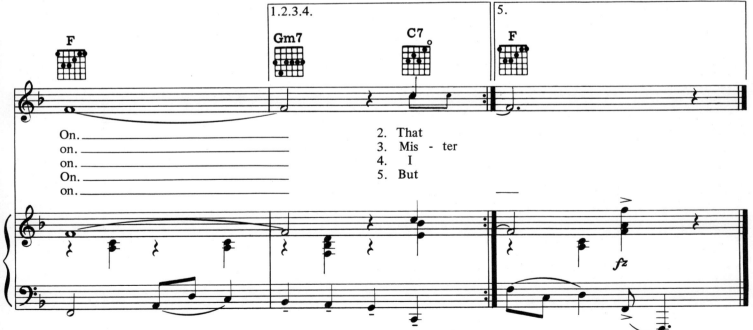

1.2.3.4. **Gm7** **C7** **5.** **F**

On. _____
on. _____
on. _____
On. _____
on. _____

2. That
3. Mis - ter
4. I
5. But

fz

I'M WALKING THE DOG

Words and music by E. M. Grimsley and W. C. Grimsley

Tacet

Don't need no one _____ to tie me down; _____
But I'm fan - cy free; _____ I don't wor-ry no - how.

I'm a - walk-in' the dog, _____ and I'm paint-in' the town. _____
So I'm walk-in' the dog, _____ all the dog will al - low. _____

Tacet

Such an eas - y life _____ I ___ nev - er knew _____ Un - til the
Such an eas - y life _____ I ___ nev - er knew; _____ I can't be -

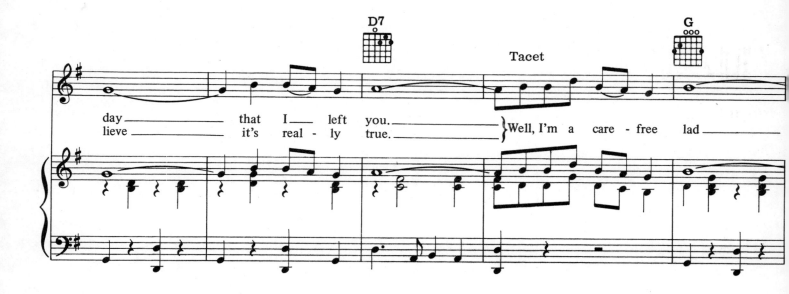

day_____ that I___ left you.___
lieve_____ it's real - ly true.___ } Well, I'm a care - free lad___

___ that seen the light. _____ I'm a - walk- in' the Dog _____ all the day and all

night. _____ 2. Well, I'm full___ of   night. _____

I REALLY DON'T WANT TO KNOW

Words by Howard Barnes Music by Don Robertson

Moderately slow

Chorus:

How man-y arms have held___ you _____ And hat-ed to let you go?_____ How man-y, how man-y, I

won- der?_____ But I Real- ly Don't Want To____ Know._____

____ How man- y lips have kissed__ you_____ And

set your soul a - glow?_____ How man- y, how

man - y, I won- der?_____ But I Real- ly Don't Want To____

154

se - cret, _____ But, dar - ling, I love you so. _____

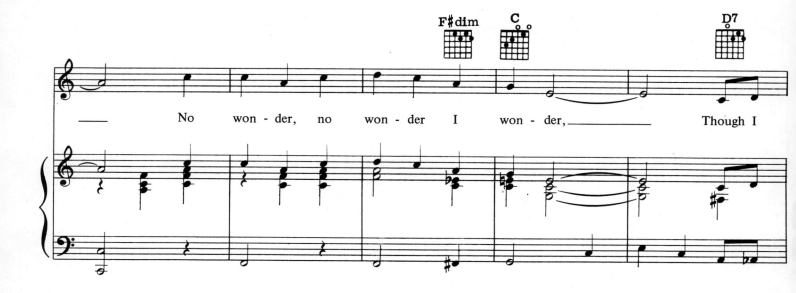

_____ No won - der, no won - der I won - der, _____ Though I

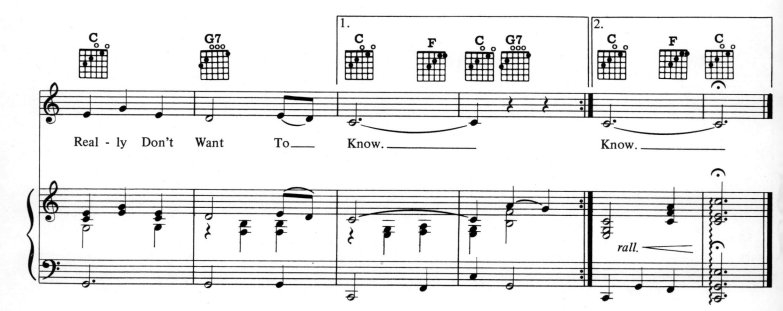

Real - ly Don't Want To___ Know. _____ Know. _____

rall.

I WALK THE LINE

Words and music by Johnny Cash

Moderately bright

Chorus:

1. I keep a close watch on this heart of mine.
2. I find it ver-y, ver-y eas-y to be true.

I keep my eyes wide o-pen all the time.
I find my-self a-lone when each day is through.

3. As sure as night is dark and day is light,
   I keep you on my mind both day and night.
   And happiness I've known proves that it's right.
   Because you're mine I Walk The Line.

4. You've got a way to keep me on your side.
   You give me cause for love that I can't hide.
   For you I know I'd even try to turn the tide.
   Because you're mine I Walk The Line.

5. I keep a close watch on this heart of mine.
   I keep my eyes wide open all the time.
   I keep the ends out for the tie that binds.
   Because you're mine I Walk The Line.

I WENT TO YOUR WEDDING

Words and music by Jessie Mae Robinson

Slowly

I Went To Your Wed-ding al-tho' I was dread-ing the thought of los-ing you. _____ The or-gan was play-ing, my poor heart kept say-ing: Your

dreams, your dreams are thru._____ You came down the aisle

wear - ing a smile, a vi - sion of love - li - ness;_____ I

ut - tered a sigh, then whis - pered good - bye, good - bye to my

hap - pi - ness._____ Your moth - er was cry - in', your

father was cry - in,' and I was cry - in', too,_____

_____ The tear - drops were fall - ing be - cause we were los - ing

you. _____ I

you. _____

IN THE MISTY MOONLIGHT

Words and music by Cindy Walker

you.   In a far a - way land, ___   On the trop - ic

sea sand, ___   If your hand's in my hand, ___   I won't ___ be

blue.   'Way up on the moun - tain, ___   Or 'way down in the

val - ley, ___ I know I'll be hap - py, ___ An - y place, an - y-

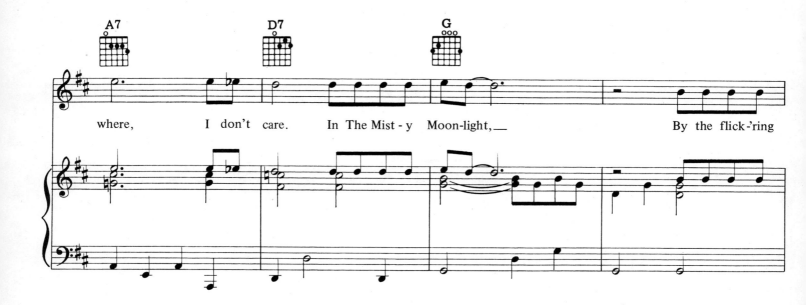

where, I don't care. In The Mist - y Moon-light, ___ By the flick-'ring

fire - light, ___ An - y place is all right, ___ long as you ___ are

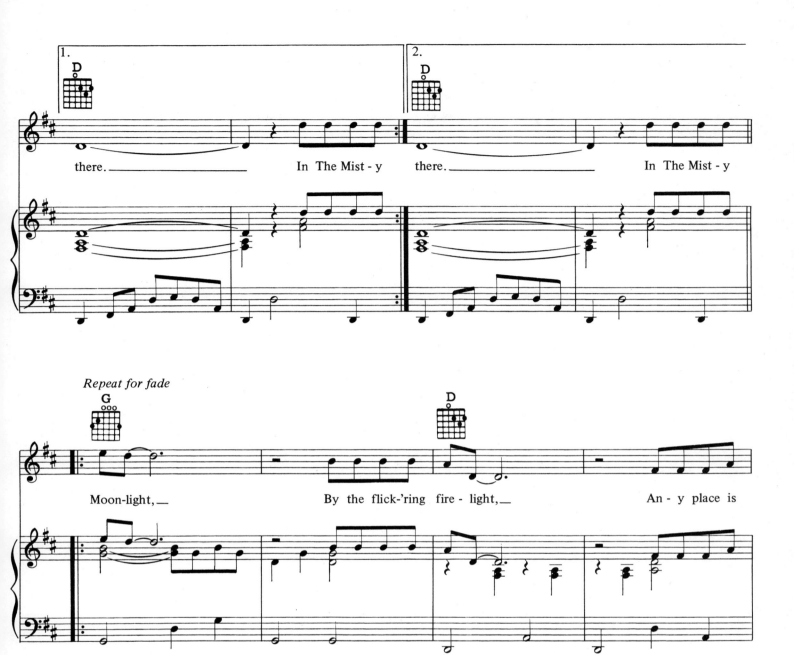

there. _____ In The Mist - y | there. _____ In The Mist - y

Repeat for fade

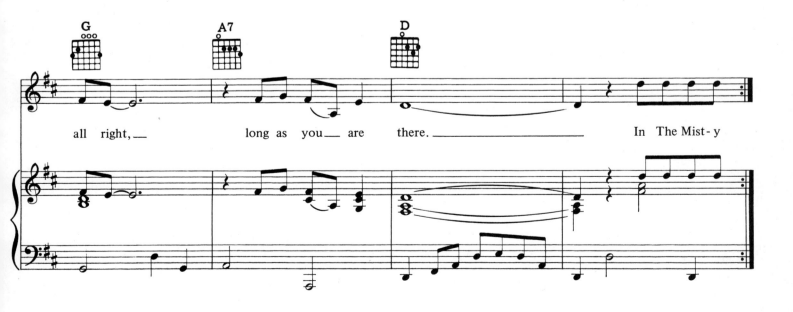

Moon-light, _____ By the flick-'ring fire - light, _____ An - y place is

all right, _____ long as you _____ are there. _____ In The Mist - y

IT WASN'T GOD WHO MADE HONKY TONK ANGELS

Words and music by J. D. Miller

1. As I sit here to-night, the juke-box play-ing
2. (It's a) shame that all the blame is on us wom-en,

The tune a-bout the wild side of life;
It's not true that on-ly you men feel the same;

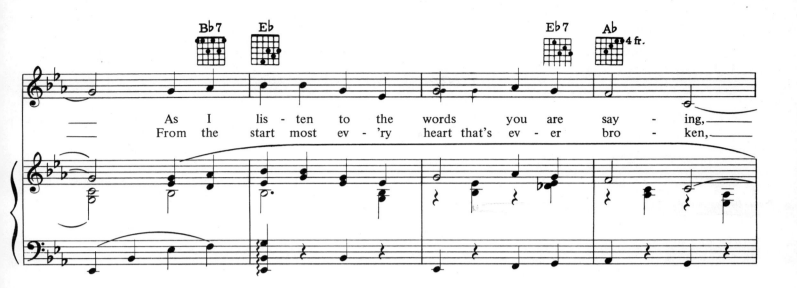

As I lis-ten to the words you are say - ing,
From the start most ev-'ry heart that's ev-er bro - ken,

It brings mem-'ries when I was a trust - ing wife.
Was be-cause there al-ways was a man to blame.

Chorus:

It Was-n't God Who Made Honk - y Tonk An - gels

As you said in the words of your song; _____

Too man-y times mar-ried men think they're still

sin - gle; _____ That has caused man-y a good girl to go

wrong._____

2. It's a wrong._____

To Verse

Fine

poco rit.

IT'S JUST A MATTER OF TIME

Words and music by Clyde Otis, Brook Benton and Belford Hendricks

in your search for for-tune and fame, what goes up must come down. I know, I know that one day you'll wake up and find that my love was a true love, It's Just A Mat-ter Of Time. Time.

I'VE GOT A TIGER BY THE TAIL

Words and music by Buck Owens and Harlan Howard

I've Got A Ti-ger By The Tail, it's plain to see;

I won't be much when you get thru' with me.

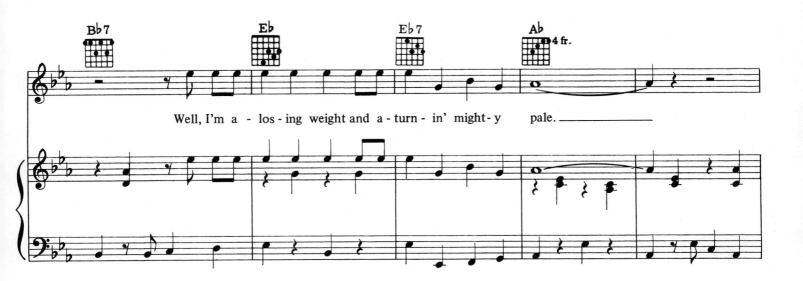

Well, I'm a - los-ing weight and a-turn-in' might-y   pale. _____

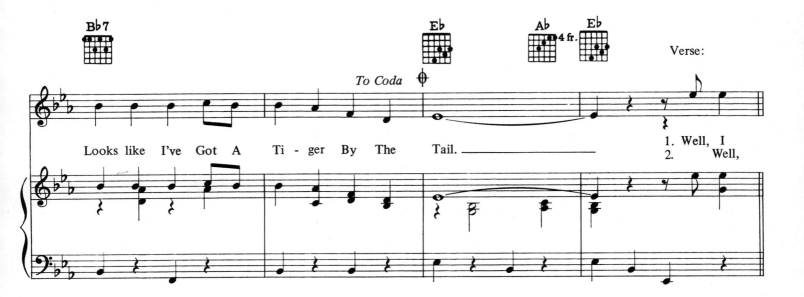

To Coda ⊕

Looks like I've Got A Ti - ger By The Tail. _____

Verse:

1. Well, I
2. Well,

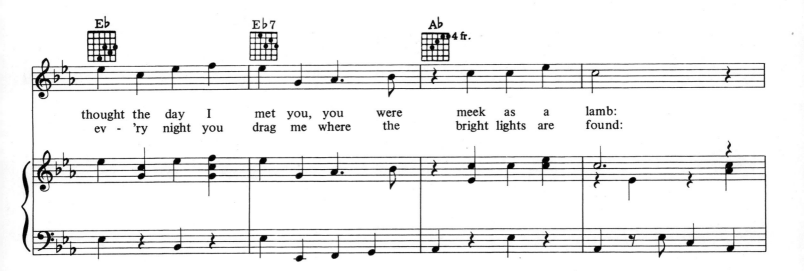

thought the day I   met you, you   were   meek as a   lamb:
ev - 'ry night you drag me where the   bright lights are found:

Just the kind, to fit my dreams and plans.
There ain't no way to slow you down.
But now, the pace we're
I'm a- bout as

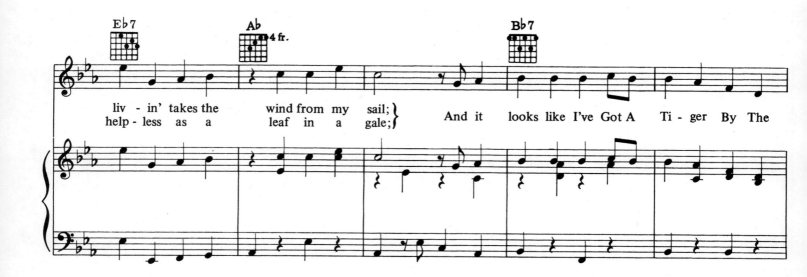

liv - in' takes the wind from my sail;
help - less as a leaf in a gale;
And it looks like I've Got A Ti - ger By The

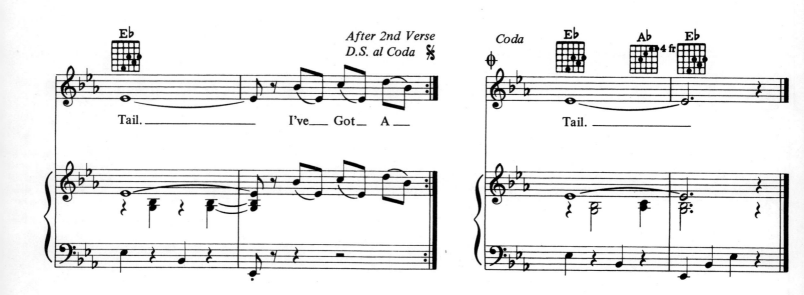

Tail. _____ I've ___ Got ___ A ___

After 2nd Verse
D.S. al Coda 𝄋

Coda

Tail. _____

JAILHOUSE ROCK

Words and music by Jerry Leiber and Mike Stoller

1. The war-den threw a par-ty in the coun-try jail. ___ The
2. ___ Spi-der Mur-phy played the ten-or sax-o-phone. ___ The
3. ___ Num-ber For-ty-sev-en said to Num-ber Three: ___

pris-on band was there and they be-gan to wail. ___ The
Lit-tle Joe was blow-in' on the slide trom-bone. ___ The
You're the cut-est jail-bird I ev-er did see. ___ I

4. The sad sack was a-sittin' on a block of stone,
   Way over in the corner weeping all alone.
   The warden said: Hey, buddy, don't you be no square.
   If you can't find a partner, use a wooden chair!
   Let's rock, etc.

5. Shifty Henry said to Bugs: For Heaven's sake,
   No one's lookin'; now's our chance to make a break.
   Bugsy turned to Shifty and he said: Nix, nix;
   I wanna stick around a while and get my kicks.
   Let's rock, etc.

JUST A LITTLE LOVIN' [WILL GO A LONG WAY]

Words and music by Zeke Clements and Eddy Arnold

1. Ev-er since that time be-gan___ love has ruled the world,
2. Don't be-lieve you real-ly know___ how much I love you,

E-ven A-dam set the pace___ and start-ed it a-whirl.
If you did you'd come on back___ and make my dreams come true. Your

I met you and now I know___ that you're the one for me,
eyes, your lips, your lov - ing kiss - es seem to lin - ger yet,

Come on back, and you will plain - ly see: _____
I'll for - give but please, don't you for - get: _____

Chorus:

Just A Lit - tle Lov - in' _____ will go a long

way, _____ And you will make me hap - py _____ the rest of my

days;_____ Put your arms a - round me,_____ then I'll be your

slave,_____ 'Cause Just A Lit - tle Lov - in'_____ will go a long

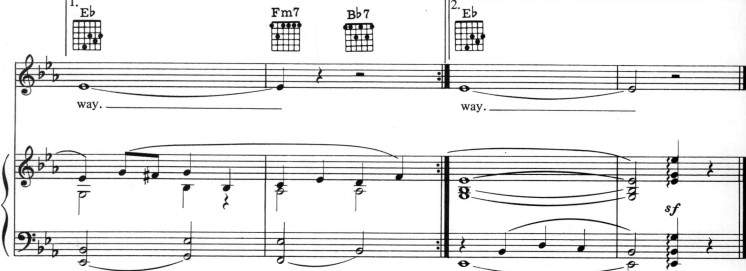

way._____ way._____

JUST WALKING IN THE RAIN

Words and music by Johnny Bragg and Robert S. Riley

Just Walk-ing In The Rain, _____ So a-lone and blue, _____

All be-cause my heart _____ Still re-mem-bers you. _____

Peo-ple come to win-dows, They al-ways stare at me,

KING OF THE ROAD

Words and music by Roger Miller

I ain't got no ci - ga - rettes.___ Ah, but two hours___ of
I don't pay no un - ion dues.___ I smoke old sto - gies
I ain't got no ci - ga - rettes.___ Ah, but two hours___ of

push - ing broom___ Buys a eight___ by twelve___ four - bit room.___ I'm a
I have found,___ Short___ but not too big a - round.___ I'm a
push - ing broom___ Buys a eight___ by twelve___ four - bit room.___ I'm a

man of means by no means, King___ Of The

1. Road.

2. Road.

To next strain *Fine*

Road.

2. I know

185

Ev - er - y en - gi - neer on ev - er - y train, ___

All of the chil - dren and all of their names, ___ And ev - er - y hand - out in

D.S. al Fine 𝄋

ev - er - y town, ___ And ev - 'ry lock that ain't locked when no one's a - round. 3. I sing

LIPSTICK ON YOUR COLLAR

Words by Edna Lewis Music by George Goehring

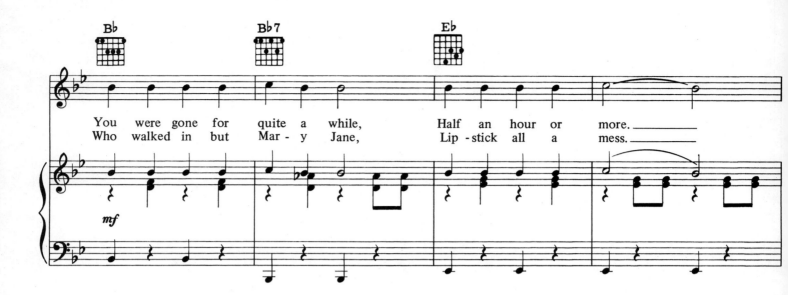

You were gone for quite a while, Half an hour or more.

Who walked in but Mar-y Jane, Lip-stick all a mess.

You came back and man, oh man, This is what I saw:

Were you smooch-in' my best friend? Guess the an-swer's yes.

Chorus:

Lip-stick On Your Col - lar told a tale on you.

188

Lip - stick On Your Col - lar___ said you were un - true._____

Bet your bot - tom dol - lar___ you and I are through 'cause

Lip - stick On Your Col - lar___ told a tale on you.

you. Told a tale on you. Told a tale on you.

LONELY AGAIN

Words and music by Jean Chapel

Slowly, with feeling

1. You told me _____ that oth-ers _____ be-
2. (You) told me _____ you want-ed _____ me

fore you _____ were fool-ish _____ to cause me _____ to
on - ly, _____ that this time _____ and this love _____ would

no arms a-round me. __ Just ____ when I'm sure ____ that my

heart ____ is se-cure, ____ and my tear - drops are dried ____ with the

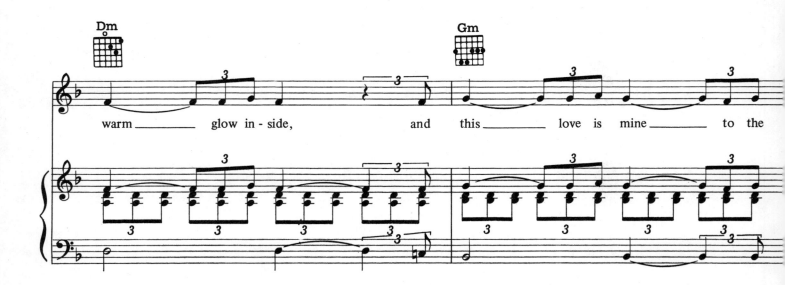

warm ____ glow in - side, and this ____ love is mine ____ to the

end＿＿＿ of the line, That's al - ways the time＿＿＿ that

I'm Lone - ly A - gain.＿＿＿

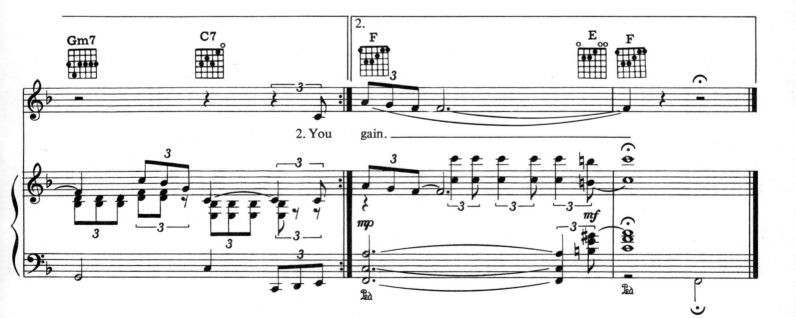

2. You gain.＿＿＿＿＿＿＿＿＿＿

LOOKING BACK

Words and music by Clyde Otis, Brook Benton and Belford Hendricks

Look - ing Back _____ o - ver my life, I can see where I caused you strife, ____ But I

know, oh, yes I know, I'd

nev-er make that same mis-take a-gain.___ Look-ing

Back ___ o-ver my deeds, I can see signs a wise man

heeds,_ And if I just had the chance, I'd

never make that same mistake again.

Once my cup was overflowing, But

I gave nothing in return.

Now I can't begin to tell you What a

LOVE ME TENDER

Words and music by Elvis Presley and Vera Matson

Verse:

1. Love Me Ten - der, love me sweet; Nev - er let me go.
2. Love Me Ten - der, love me long; Take me to your heart.
3. Love Me Ten - der, love me dear; Tell me you are mine.

You have made my life com - plete, And I love you so.
For it's there that I be - long, And we'll nev - er part.
I'll be yours through all the years, Till the end of time.

4. When at last my dreams come true,
Darling, this I know:
Happiness will follow you
Everywhere you go.

LOVING HER WAS EASIER THAN ANYTHING I'LL EVER DO AGAIN

Words and music by Kris Kristofferson

I have seen the morn-ing burn-ing gold-en on the moun-tain in the
Wak-ing in the morn-ing to the feel-ing of her fin-gers on my

skies;
skin;

Ach-ing with the feel-ing of the
Wip-ing out the trac-es of the

free - dom of an ea - gle when she flies;
peo - ple and the plac - es that I've been;

Turn - ing on the world, the way she smiled up - on my soul as I lay dy -
Teach - ing me that yes - ter - day was some - thing that I nev - er thought of try -

ing;
ing;

Heal - ing as the col - ors in the sun - shine and the shad - ows of her
Talk - ing of to - mor - row and the mon - ey, love and time we had to

eyes.

spend.

Lov - ing Her Was Eas - i - er Than An - y - thing I'll Ev - er Do A -

gain.   Com - ing close to - geth - er, with a   feel - ing that I'd nev - er known be -

fore,   in my time;   She ain't a - shamed to be a

wom - an or a - fraid   to be a   friend._____

I don't know the an-swer to the eas - y way she o-pened ev - ery door   in my

mind;   But dream-ing was as eas-y as be - liev - ing it was nev - er gon - na

end; _____   And Lov - ing Her Was Eas - i - er Than

An - y -thing I'll Ev - er Do A - gain.

rall.

203

MAKE THE WORLD GO AWAY

Words and music by Hank Cochran

And Make The World Go A - way.

And Make The World Go A - way.

Chorus:

Make The World Go A - way,

And get it off my shoul-ders,

Say the things you used to say,

And Make The World Go A -

1. way.

2. I'm sor-ry if I

2. way.

MAY THE BIRD OF PARADISE FLY UP YOUR NOSE

Words and music by Neal Merritt

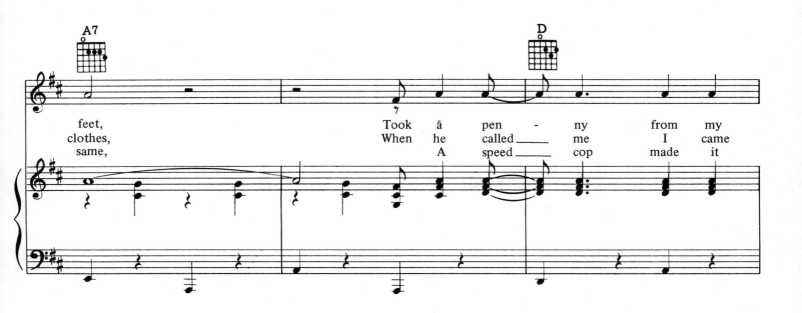

feet,
clothes,
same,

Took a pen - ny from my
When he called ___ me I came
A speed ___ cop made it

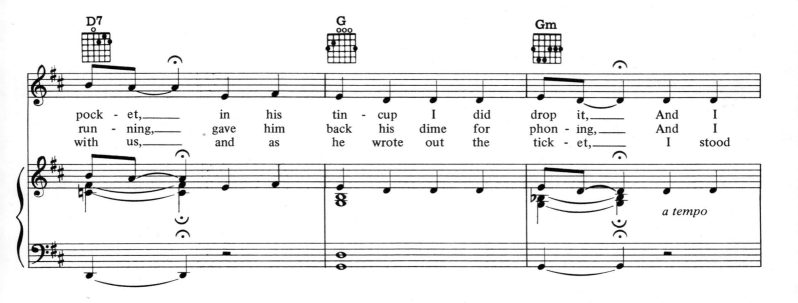

pock - et, ___ in his tin - cup I did drop it, ___ And I
run - ning, ___ gave him back his dime for phon - ing, ___ And I
with us, ___ and as he wrote out the tick - et, ___ I stood

a tempo

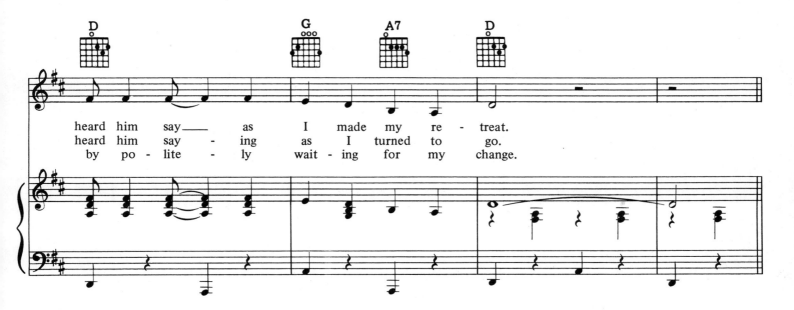

heard him say ___ as I made my re - treat.
heard him say - ing as I turned to go.
by po - lite - ly wait - ing for my change.

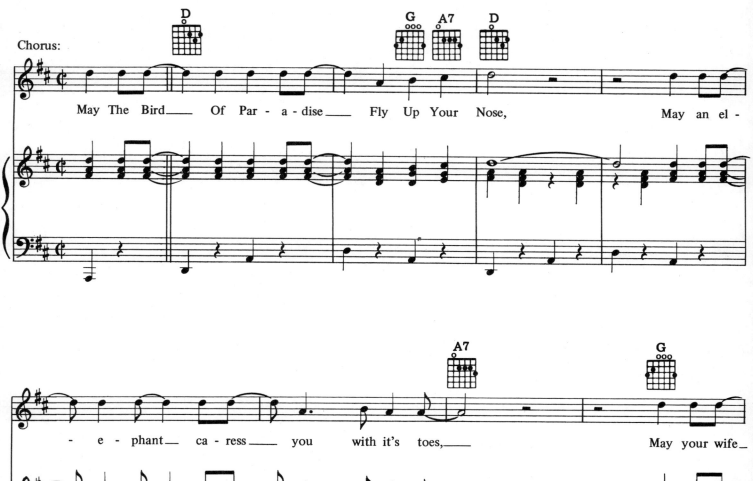

Chorus:

May The Bird___ Of Par - a - dise___ Fly Up Your Nose, May an el -

- e - phant___ ca - ress___ you with it's toes,___ May your wife___

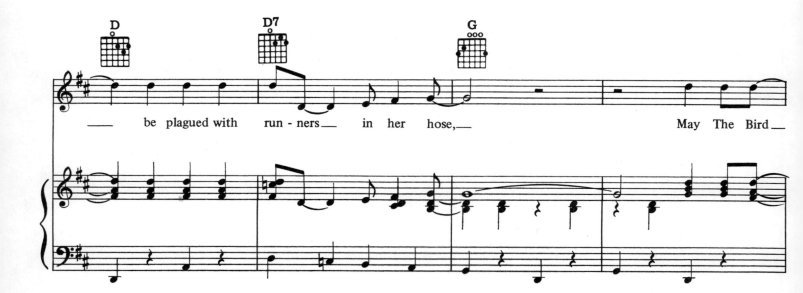

___ be plagued with run - ners___ in her hose,___ May The Bird

Me and Bobby McGee

Words and music by Kris Kristofferson and Fred Foster

rained; Took us all the way to New Or - leans. _____
done, And ev - 'ry night she kept me from the cold. _____

_____ I took my har - poon out of my dirt - y, red ban -
Then some - where near Sa - lin - as, Lord, I let her slip a -

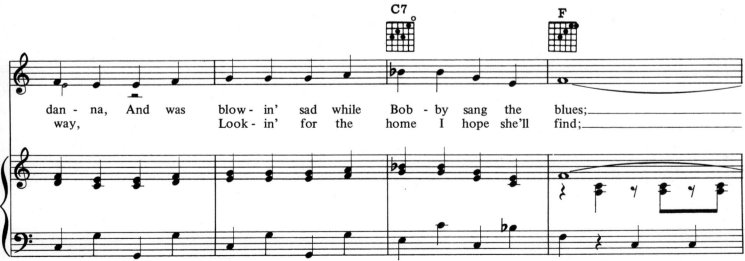

dan - na, And was blow - in' sad while Bob - by sang the blues; _____
way, Look - in' for the home I hope she'll find; _____

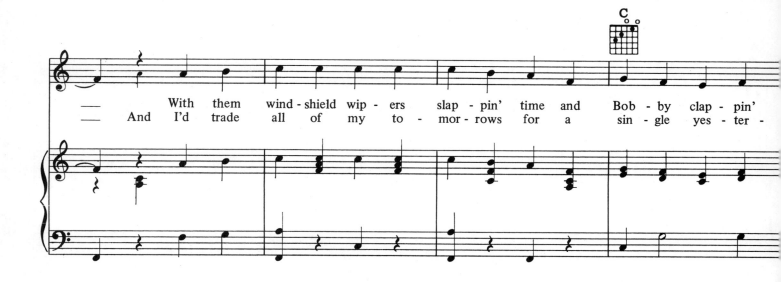

With them wind-shield wip-ers slap-pin' time and Bob-by clap-pin'
And I'd trade all of my to-mor-rows for a sin-gle yes-ter-

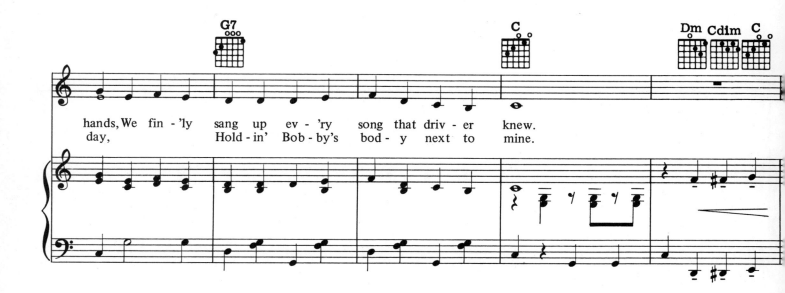

hands, We fin-'ly sang up ev-'ry song that driv-er knew.
day, Hold-in' Bob-by's bod-y next to mine.

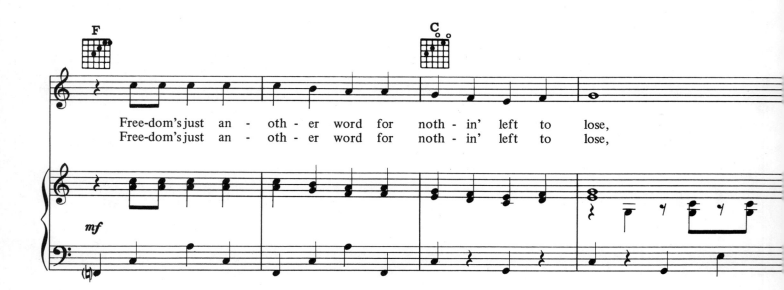

Free-dom's just an-oth-er word for noth-in' left to lose,
Free-dom's just an-oth-er word for noth-in' left to lose,

ME AND JESUS

Words and music by Tom T. Hall

Je - sus got our own thing go - ing, ___

We don't need an - y - bod - y to tell us what it's all a -

to next strain

Fine

bout. _____

1. I know a bout. _____
2. Je - sus
3. We can't af -

ritard.

man once was a sin - ner, ___
brought me ___ through all of my trou - bles, ___
ford an - y fan - cy preach - in', ___

I know a man that once was a drunk;
Je - sus brought me through all of my trials;
We can't af - ford an - y fan - cy church;

I know a man
Je - sus brought me through all of my
We can't af - ford an - y fan - cy

los - er, But he went out one day and made an
heart - aches, And I know one that Je - sus ain't a -
sing - in', But you know Je - sus got a lot of poor

al - tar out of a stump.
gon - na for - sake me now.
peo - ple out a - do - in' his work.

After 3rd verse
D.S. al Fine

Me And

216

MY ELUSIVE DREAMS

Words and music by Curly Putman and Billy Sherrill

Moderately

Verse:

1. You fol-lowed me to Tex-as, you fol-lowed me to U-tak, We
2. (You) had my child in Mem-phis, then I heard of work in Nash-ville, But We
3. ___ Now we've left A-las-ka be-cause there was no gold mine, But

did-n't find it there, so we moved on.___ Then you
did-n't find it there, so we moved on.___ to a
this time on-ly two of us moved on.___ And

went with me to A-la-bam', Things looked good in Bir-ming-ham, We
small farm in Ne-bras-ka,____ to a gold mine in A-las-ka, We
now all we have is each oth-er and a lit - tle mem-o-ry to

did-n't find it there, so we moved on._____
did-n't find it there, so we moved on._____
cling to, and____ still you won't let me go on a-lone.

Chorus:
Tacet

I know you're tired of fol-low-ing My E-lu-sive Dreams and schemes,____

for they're on - ly fleet-ing things, My E-lu-sive Dreams.__ 2.You Dreams.
3.____

1.,2.
3.

NOBODY WINS

Words and music by Kris Kristofferson

long. _____ And it's too late to try to save _____ what might have been. _____
try. _____ 'Cause it's a shame to make the same _____ mis - takes a - gain _____

_____ and a - gain. It's o - ver, No - bod - y Wins.

Make be - liev - ing in for - _____

We've gone too far, too long, too far a - part;

The lov-ing was eas - y,_____ It's the liv-ing that's hard._____

And there's no need to stay to see_____ the way it ends,____

It's o - ver, No - bod - y Wins,___

It's o - ver, No - bod - y Wins.___

rall.

NORTH TO ALASKA

Words and music by Mike Phillips

Big Sam left Se - at - tle in the year of nine - ty - two, With
George turned to Sam with his gold in his hand, Said,

George Pratt, his part - ner, and broth - er Bil - ly too; They
"Sam, you're a - look - in' at a lone - ly, lone - ly man; I'd

North-ern Lights a run-nin' wild in the Land of the Mid-night Sun, Yes,
build for my Jen-ny a hon - ey-moon home, Be -

Sam Mc-Cord was a might-y man in the year of nine-teen - one.
low that old White Moun - tain, just a lit-tle south-east of Nome."

Chorus:

Where the riv - er is wind - in', big nug - gets they're find - in',

North To A - las - ka, Go north, the rush is on. on.

224

OKIE FROM MUSKOGEE

Words and music by Merle Haggard and Roy Edward Burris

Verse:

1. We don't smoke ma-ri-jua-na in Mus-ko-gee,___
2. We don't make a par-ty out of lov-ing,___
3. boots are still in style if a man needs foot-wear,___

And we don't take our trips on L. S.
But we like hold-ing hands and pitch-ing
Beads and Ro-man San-dals won't be

Bb7

D.
woo.
seen.

And we don't burn our draft cards down on
We don't let our hair grow long and
Foot - ball's still the rough - est thing on

Main Street,
shag - gy
cam - pus,

But we like liv - ing
Like the hip - pies out in
And the kids here still re -

Eb

Chorus:

right and be - ing free. ____
San Fran - cis - co do. ____
spect the Col - lege Dean. ____

And I'm

Eb

proud to be an O - kie From Mus - ko - gee;

A place where e - ven squares can have a ball.___

Bb7

___ We still wave Ol' Glo - ry down at the

Court House, White light - ning's still the

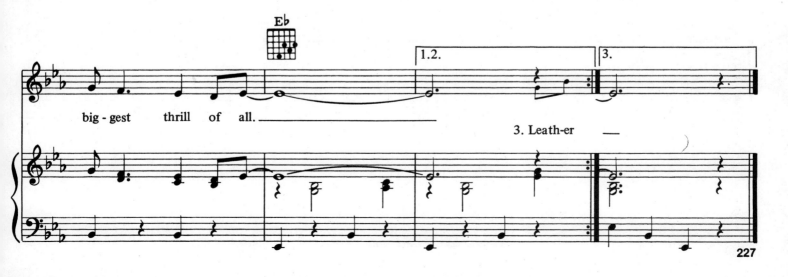

Eb

big - gest thrill of all._____

1. 2.

3.

3. Leath-er ___

OLD DOGS, CHILDREN AND WATERMELON WINE

Words and music by Tom T. Hall

(Spoken) 1. How old do you think I am? He said. I said, well I didn't know. He said, I turned sixty five about eleven months ago. (Sung) I was

3. Ever had a drink of watermelon wine? He asked.
   He told me all about it though I didn't answer back.
   Ain't but three things in this world that's worth a solitary dime,
   But Old Dogs, Children And Watermelon Wine.

4. He said women think about theyselves when menfolk ain't around,
   And friends are hard to find when they discover that you down.
   He said I tried it all when I was young and in my natural prime;
   Now it's Old Dogs, Children And Watermelon Wine.

5. Old dogs care about you even when you make mistakes.
   God bless little children while they're still too young to hate.
   When he moved away, I found my pen and copied down that line
   'Bout old dogs and children and watermelon wine.

6. I had to catch a plane up to Atlanta that next day,
   As I left for my room I saw him pickin' up my change.
   That night I dreamed in peaceful sleep of shady summertime
   Of old dogs and children and watermelon wine.

Glen Campbell

Conway Twitty   Loretta Lynn

Johnny Cash

Jim Reeves

Johnny Tillotson

PAPER ROSES

Words by Janice Torre Music by Fred Spielman

Moderately Slow with Expresssion

Verse:

1. I re-al-ize the way your eyes de-ceived me_____ With
(Boy) 2. (Your) pret-ty lips look warm and so ap-peal-ing,_____ They
(Girl) 3. (I) thought that you would be a per-fect lov-er,_____ You

ten-der looks that I mis-took for love;_____ (Girl) So
seem to have the sweet-ness of a rose;_____ (Boy) So
seemed so full of sweet-ness at the start;_____ But

But

take a - way the flow - ers that you gave me_____ And
throw a - way the flow - ers that I gave you_____ I'll
when you give a kiss there is no feel - ing,_____ It's
like a big red rose that's made of pa - per,_____ There

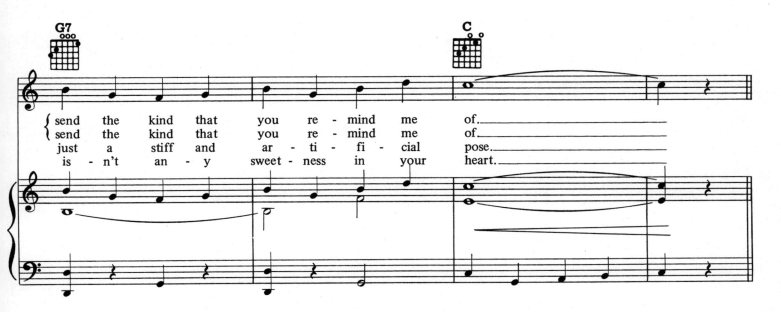

send the kind that you re - mind me of._____
send the kind that you re - mind me of._____
just a stiff and ar - ti - fi - cial pose._____
is - n't an - y sweet - ness in your heart._____

Chorus:

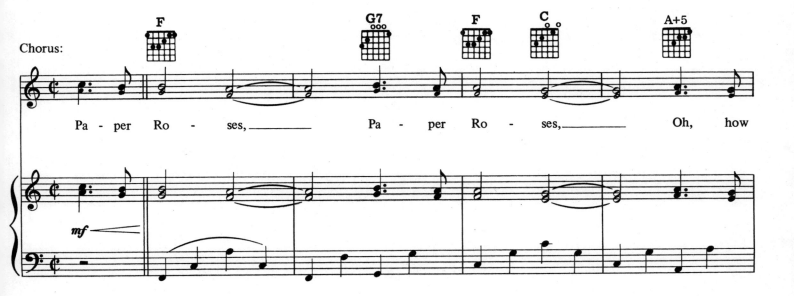

Pa - per Ro - ses,_____ Pa - per Ro - ses,_____ Oh, how

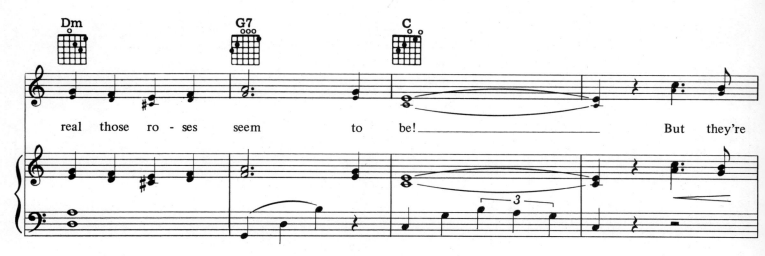

real those ro - ses seem to be!_____ But they're

on - ly_____ im - i - ta - tion_____ Like your

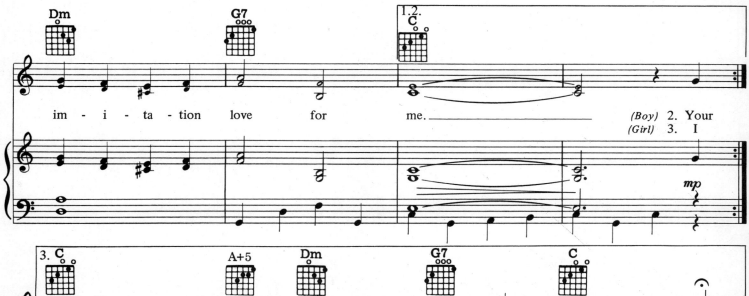

im - i - ta - tion love for me._____ *(Boy)* 2. Your
(Girl) 3. I

me._____ Like your im - i - ta - tion love for me._____

PLEASE DON'T TELL ME HOW THE STORY ENDS

Words and music by Kris Kristofferson

This could be our last good night to-geth-er;_____ We may nev-er
See the way our shad-ows come to-geth-er;_____ Soft-er than your

pass this way a-gain;_____ Just let me en-joy it till it's
fin-gers on my skin;_____ Some-day these may be all____ we re-

o-ver, or for-ev-er;} Please Don't Tell Me How The Sto-ry
mem-ber of each oth-er;}

PLEASE HELP ME I'M FALLING [IN LOVE WITH YOU]

Words and music by Don Robertson and Hal Blair

238

RELEASE ME

Words and music by Eddie Miller, Dub Williams and Robert Yount

Moderately slow

1. Please Re - lease Me, let me go, _____
2. I have found a new love, dear, _____
3. Please Re - lease Me, can't you see, _____

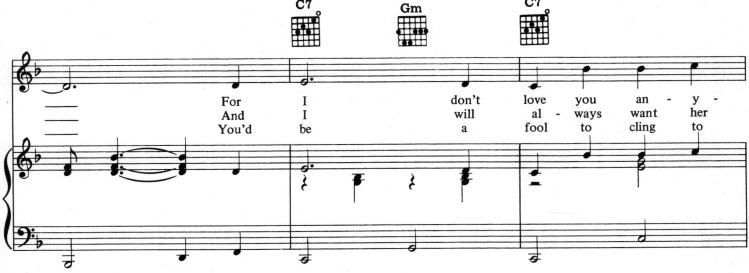

For I don't love you an - y - _____
And I will al - ways want her
You'd be a fool to cling to

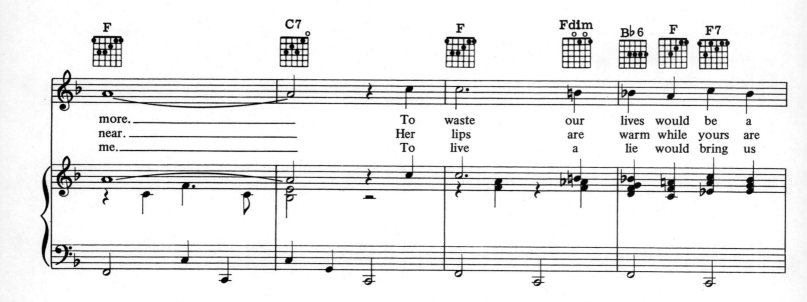

more. / near. / me.

To waste our lives would be a / Her lips are warm while yours are / To live a lie would bring us

sin, / cold, / pain,

Re - lease Me and let me love a - / Re - lease Me, my dar - ling, let me / So Re - lease Me and let me love a -

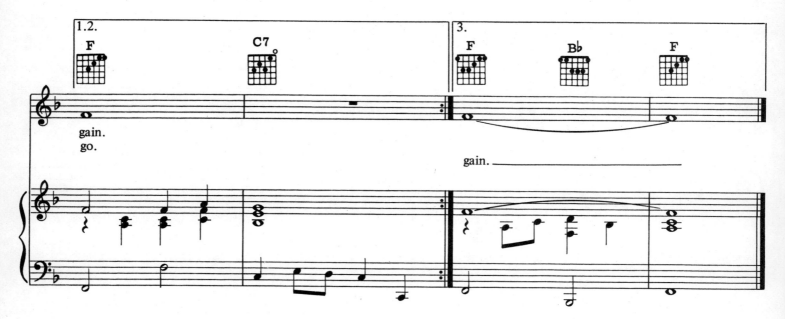

1.2.

gain. / go.

3.

gain.

SEND ME THE PILLOW YOU DREAM ON

Words and music by Hank Locklin

Chorus:
Send Me The Pil-low That You Dream On,

Don't you know that I still care for you?

Send Me The Pil-low__ That You Dream On,_____ So,

dar-ling, I can dream on it too._____ { 1. Each
{ (2. I've)

night while I'm sleep-ing, oh, so lone-ly,_____ I'll
wait-ed so long for you to write me,_____ But

share your love in dreams that once were true; _____ Send Me The
just a mem-'ry's all that's left of you; _____

Pil - low__ That You Dream On, _____ So, dar - ling, I can

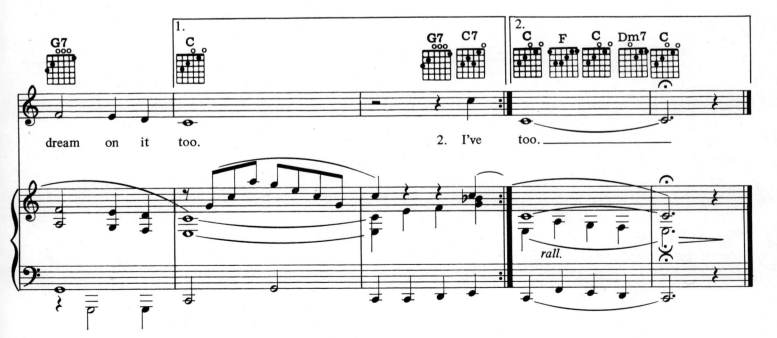

1.
dream on it too.

2. I've too. _____

rall.

SIXTEEN TONS

Words and music by Merle Travis

Moderate tempo

Verse:

1. Some peo - ple say a man is made out of mud, ___ A
2. (I was) born one morn - in' when the sun did - n't shine, ___ I
3. (I was) born one morn - in', it was driz - zl - ing rain, ___ A
4. (If you) see me com - in', bet - ter ___ step a - side, ___ A

poor man's made out of mus - cle and blood,
picked up my shov - el and I walked to the mine, I load - ed
Fight - in' and trou - ble are my mid - dle name ___ I was
lot - ta men did - n't, a lot - ta men died,

Em   Am

Mus - cle and blood and skin and bones, _____ A
Six - teen Tons of num - ber nine coal, And the
raised in a cane - brake by an ole ma - ma lion, Cain't no
One fist of i - ron, the oth - er of steel, If the

C7   Em

mind that's _____ weak and a back that's strong. You load
straw - boss _____ said, "Well - a bless my soul." You load
high - toned _____ wom - an make me walk the line. You load
right one don't - a get you, then the left one will. You load

Chorus:
Em

Six - teen Tons, what do you get? _____ An - oth - er day old - er and

deep - er in debt.___ Saint Pe - ter, don't you call me 'cause

I can't go,___ I owe___ my soul to the com - pa - ny store.___

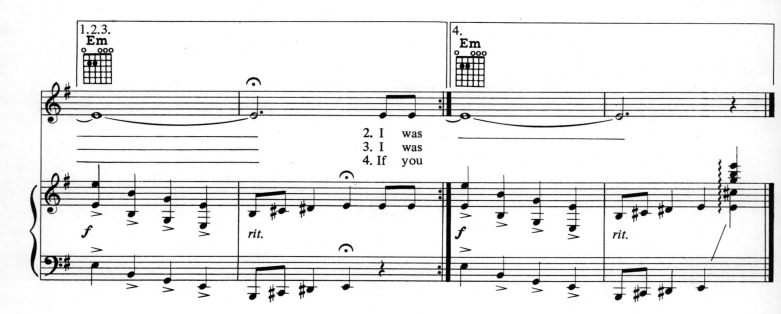

1. 2. 3.

2. I was
3. I was
4. If you

f *rit.*

4.

f *rit.*

SKIP A ROPE

Words and music by Jack Moran and Glenn D. Tubb

Skip A Rope!   Skip A Rope!

Oh, lis-ten to the chil-dren while they play.

Now, ain't it kind-a fun-ny what the chil-dren say. Skip A
(last time: sad ___)

Rope.

1. ___
2. The

1. Teach-ers are on strike, no school to - day; ___
2. Vi - et - nam war goes on and on; ___

The

To next strain

Fine

248

After last verse, D.S. al Fine 𝄌

All we got to do is Skip A Rope and play. _____

draft came and took a - way my broth - er John. _____

When we go back, you know what we can do, _____

Chil-dren in Bi - af - ra live in pov - er - ty; _____ We

Start a lit - tle ri - ot like the col - lege kids do. } Skip A

watch them starve on our col - or T. V. }

3. Jews hate Arabs, Arabs hate Jews.
   We hear it every night on the evening news.
   Wonder what it's like to get real high,
   When I grow up, I think I'm gonna try.

SLOW POKE

Words and music by Pee Wee King, Redd Stewart and Chilton Price

nev - er seem to hur - ry, you're a Slow Poke.

Time means noth - in' to you, I wait and then,

late a - gain, Eight o - clock, nine o - clock, quar - ter to ten.

Why should I lin - ger ev - 'ry time you snap your fin - ger, Lit - tle

Slow Poke, Why can't you has - ten when you

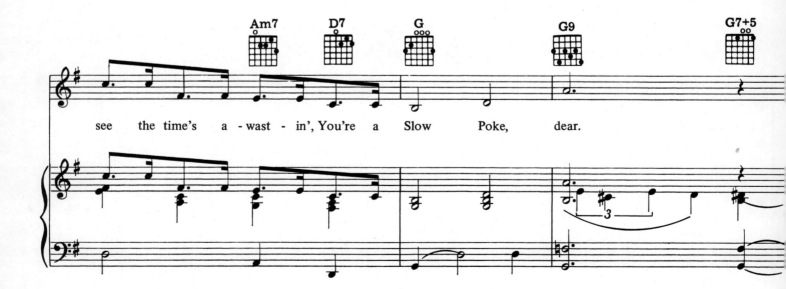

see the time's a - wast - in', You're a Slow Poke, dear.

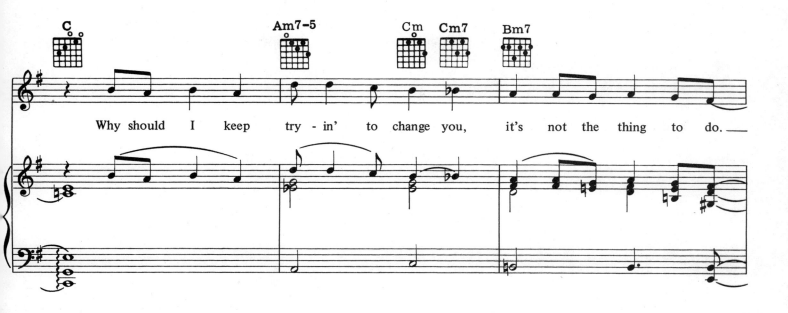

Why should I keep try - in' to change you, it's not the thing to do.

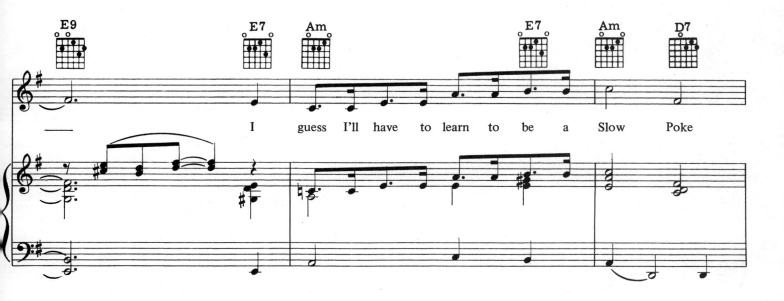

I guess I'll have to learn to be a Slow Poke

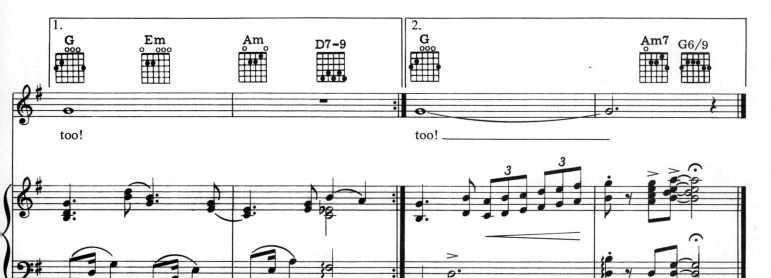

1.
too!

2.
too!

STAND BY YOUR MAN

Words and music by Tammy Wynette and Billy Sherrill

Some - times___ it's hard___ to be a wom - an,___

But if___ you love him,___ you'll for - give him,___

giv - ing all your love to just one man.___

e - ven though he's hard to un - der - stand.

Stand By Your Man, And show the world you love him,

Keep giv-ing all the love you can,_____

Stand By Your Man._____

SUNDAY MORNIN' COMIN' DOWN

Words and music by Kris Kristofferson

Then I fum - bled through my clos - et for my clothes and found my clean-est___ dirt-y
Then I crossed the emp - ty street and caught the Sun - day smell of some-one___ fry-in'

shirt;   And I shaved my face, and combed my hair, and
chick-en;___ And it

stum-bled down the stair to meet the day._____ I'd

took me back to some-thin' that I'd lost some-how some-where a - long the way.

On the Sun - day morn - in' side - walks, wish - in', Lord, that I was

stoned, 'Cause there's some-thing in a Sun - day

makes a bod - y feel a - lone; And there's noth - in' short of

3. In the park I saw a daddy with a laughing little girl that he was swingin';
   And I stopped beside a Sunday School and listened to the song that they were singin';
   Then I headed back for home, and somewhere far away a lonely bell was ringin';
   And it echoed thru the canyon like the disappearing dreams of yesterday.

TEARS ON MY PILLOW

Words and music by Gene Autry and Fred Rose

Chorus: Tears On My Pil-low each morn - ing, _____ I cry when I dream a-bout you. _____ When I should be sleep-ing, I

To Verse   F   F#dim   C7 | *Fine*   F   B♭   F   Gm7   F

you.

you. _____

Verse: F   E7   E♭7   D7   G7   F#7   G7   C7

We were so hap-py when love lin-gered on,   Back in the

F   C7   F   E7   E♭7   D7

sweet -used-to- be; _____   But now I'm so lone-ly be-

G7   F#7   G7   Dm7   G7   C7   *D.S. al Fine*

cause you are gone,   Leav-ing a sad mem-o-ry. _____   I'm

264

THAT LUCKY OLD SUN

Words by Haven Gillespie Music by Beasley Smith

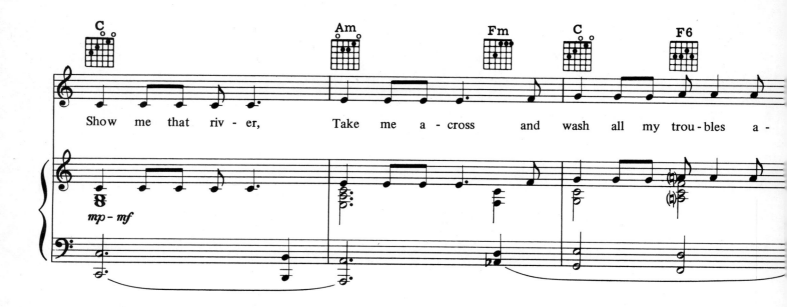

Show me that riv-er, Take me a-cross and wash all my trou-bles a-

way. Like That Luck-y Old Sun, give me noth-in' to do but

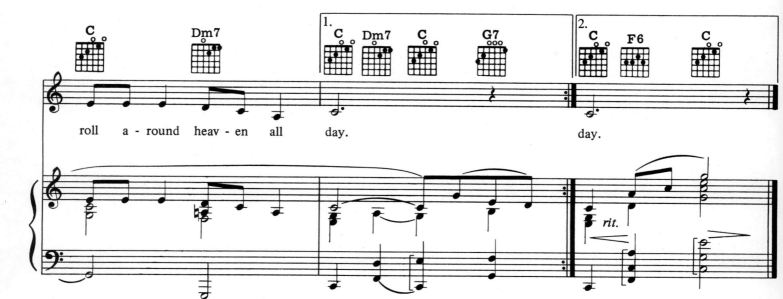

roll a-round heav-en all day.   day.

THE GREEN LEAVES OF SUMMER

Words by Paul Francis Webster Music by Dimitri Tiomkin

call - in' me home. _____ It was good _____ to be
call - in' me home. _____ It was good _____ to be

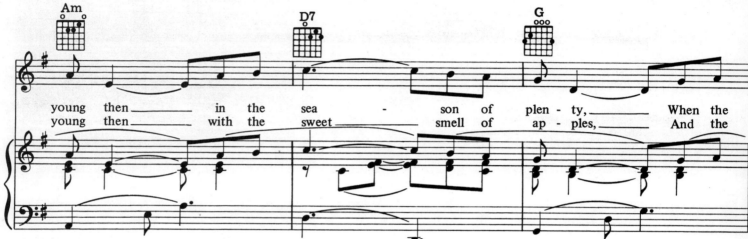

young then _____ in the sea - son of plen - ty, _____ When the
young then _____ with the sweet _____ smell of ap - ples, _____ And the

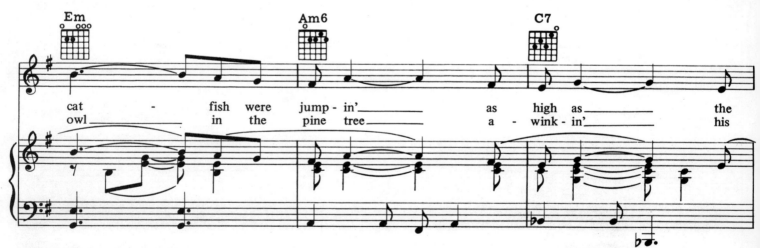

cat - fish were jump - in' _____ as high as _____ the
owl _____ in the pine tree _____ a - wink - in' _____ his

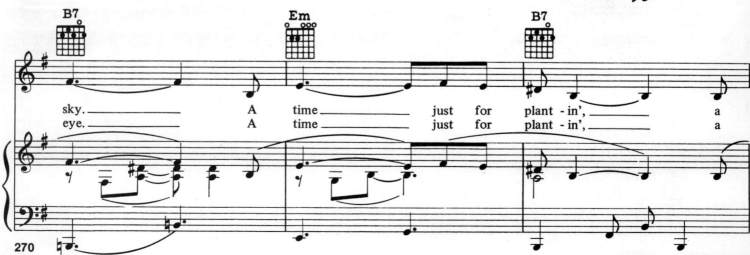

sky. _____ A time _____ just for plant - in', _____ a
eye. _____ A time _____ just for plant - in', _____ a

THE LETTER

Words and music by Wayne Carson Thompson

I don't care how much mon-ey I got-ta spend, Got to get back__ to my

ba - by.__ Lone - ly days are gone,__ I'm a-go-in' home,__ My

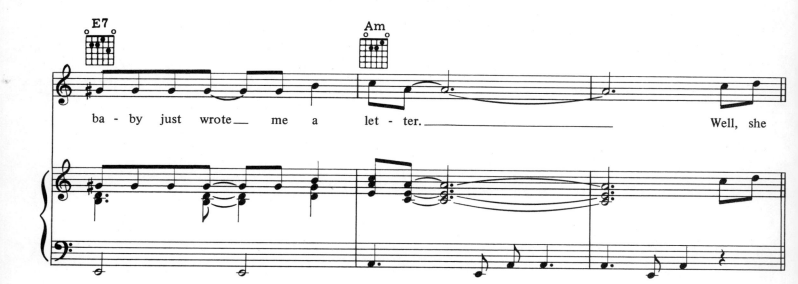

ba - by just wrote__ me a let - ter._____ Well, she

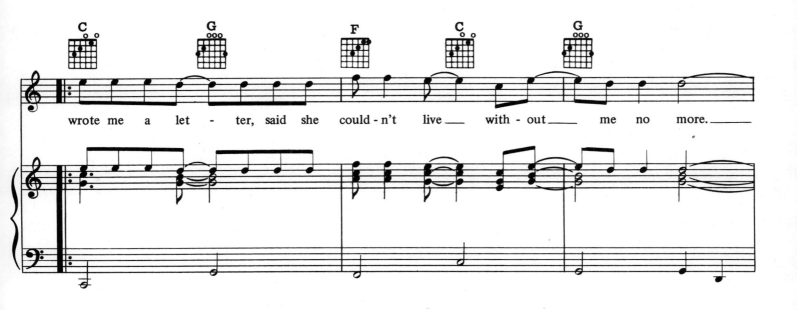

wrote me a let - ter, said she could-n't live___ with-out___ me no more.___

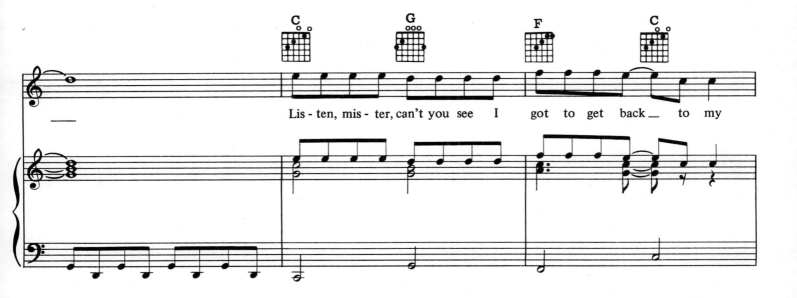

___ Lis - ten, mis - ter, can't you see I got to get back___ to my

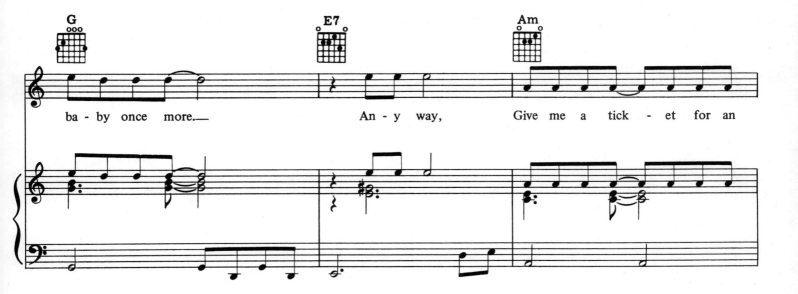

ba - by once more.___ An - y way, Give me a tick - et for an

air - plane, Ain't got time___ to take the fast - est train.

Lone - ly days are gone,___ I'm a - go - in' home,___ My ba - by just wrote___ me a

let - ter.___ Well, she let - ter.___ My ba - by just wrote___ me a let - ter.___ My

Repeat for fade

THE PURPLE PEOPLE EATER

Words and music by Sheb Wooley

278

THE RACE IS ON

Words and music by Don Rollins

Bright country tempo

1. I feel tears well-in' up cold and deep in-side like
2. (One day I) ven-tured in love, nev-er once sus-pect-in' what the

my heart's sprung a big break; And a stab of lone-li-ness
fi-nal re-sult would be. How I lived in fear of wak-ing

sharp and pain-ful that I may nev-er shake. Now,
up each morn-ing and find-ing that you're gone from me. There's

you might say that I was tak-ing it hard since you wrote me off with a
ache and pain in my heart, for to-day was the one that I ha-ted to

call; But don't you wa-ger that I'll hide my sor-row when I may
face. Some-bod-y new came up to win her and I came

break right down and bawl.
out in sec-ond place.

Now The Race Is On and here comes

pride____ up the back-stretch..... Heart-aches are go-ing to the in-side....

THE THREE BELLS

English Lyrics by Bert Reisfeld; music and French lyric by Jean Villard (Gilles)

1. There's a vil - lage hid - den deep in the val - ley, A - mong the
2. There's a vil - lage hid - den deep in the val - ley, Be - neath the
3. From the vil - lage hid - den deep in the val - ley, One rain - y
1. _____ Vil - la - ge au fond de la val - lé - e, Comme é - ga -

pine trees half for - lorn, And there on a sun - ny morn - ing
moun - tains high a - bove, And there, twen - ty years there - af - ter,
morn - ing dark and gray, A soul winged its way to heav - en,
ré, pres qu'i - gno - re, Voi - ci, dans la nuit é - toi - lé - e, Qu'un

Lit - tle Jim - my Brown was born; So his par - ents brought him to the
Jim - my was to meet his love. Man - y friends were gath - ered in the
Jim - my Brown had passed a - way. Si - lent peo - ple gath - ered in the
nou - veau né nous est don - né; Jean Fran - çois Ni - cot____ il se

chap - el, When he was on - ly one day old, And the priest blessed the lit - tle
chap - el, And man - y tears of joy were shed, In____ June on a Sun - day
chap - el, To say fare - well to their old friend, Whose____ life had been like a
nom - me, Il est jouf - flu, tendre et ro - sé, A l'é - gli - se, beau pe - tit

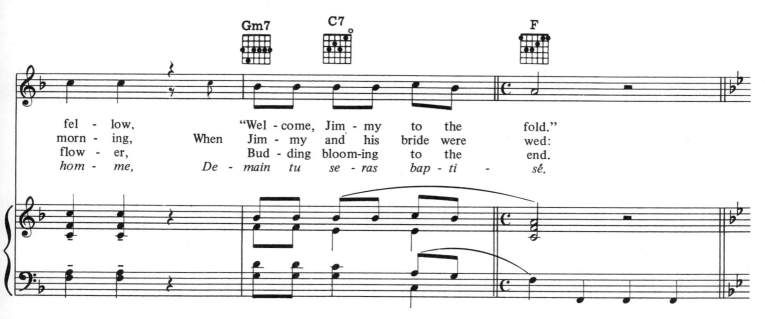

fel - low, "Wel - come, Jim - my to the fold."
morn - ing, When Jim - my and his bride were wed:
flow - er, Bud - ding bloom - ing to the end.
hom - me, De - main tu se - ras bap - ti - sé.

Prayed for guid-ance from a - bove,
Prayed for guid-ance from a - bove,
Prayed for guid-ance from a - bove,
U - ne fleur qui s'ouvre au jour;

"Lead us not in - to temp-
"Lead us not in - to temp-
"Lead us not in - to temp-
A peine, à peine, u - ne

ta - tion, Bless this hour of med - i - ta - tion, Guide him with e - ter - nal
ta - tion, Bless, Oh Lord, this cel - e - bra - tion, May their lives be filled with
ta - tion, May his soul find the Sal - va - tion Of Thy great e - ter - nal
flam - me en - cor fai - ble qui ré - cla - me Pro - tec - tion ten - dresse a -

love.
love.
mour.

2. There's a
3. From the
1. Vil - love.
mour.

D.S. al Fine   *Fine*

THERE GOES MY EVERYTHING

Words and music by Dallas Frazier

Moderately slow

Verse:

1. I hear foot-steps slow-ly walk-ing, _____ As they gent-ly walk a-
2. (As my) mem-'ry turns back the pag-es, _____ I can see the hap-py

cross___ a lone-ly floor, _____ And a voice___ is soft-ly
years___ we had be-fore. _____ Now the love___ that kept this old heart

say - ing: ____ "Dar-ling this will be good - bye ____ for - ev - er - more."
beat - ing ____ Has been shat-tered by the clos - ing of the door. ____

Chorus:
There goes my rea - son for liv - ing, There goes the one of my

dreams, ____ There goes my on - ly pos - ses - sion,

There Goes My Ev - 'ry - thing.   2. As my thing. ____

THERE'LL BE PEACE IN THE VALLEY FOR ME

Words and music by Thomas A. Dorsey

Moderato

Verse:

1. I am tir - ed and wea - ry but I must toil
2. (There the) flow'rs will be bloom - ing, the grass will be
3. (There the) bear will be gen - tle, the wolf will be
4. (No) head - aches or heart - aches or mis - un - der -

F

Bb

on Till the Lord comes to call me a - way,
green, And the skies will be clear and se - rene,
tame, And the lion will lay down with the Lamb,
stands, No con - fu - sion or trou - ble won't be,

F   G7   C7   G7

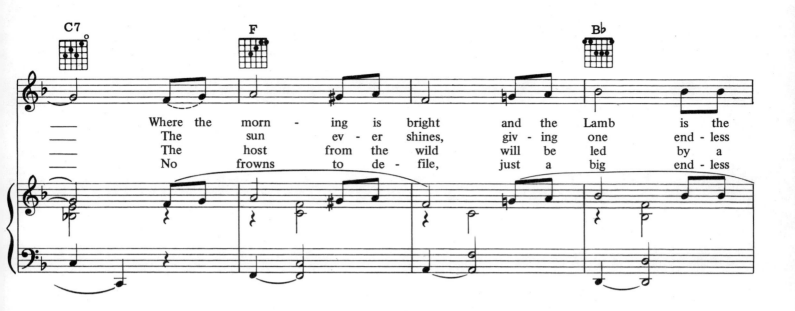

Where the morn - ing is bright, and the Lamb is the
The sun ev - er shines, giv - ing one is end - less
The host from the wild will be led by a
No frowns to de - file, just a big end - less

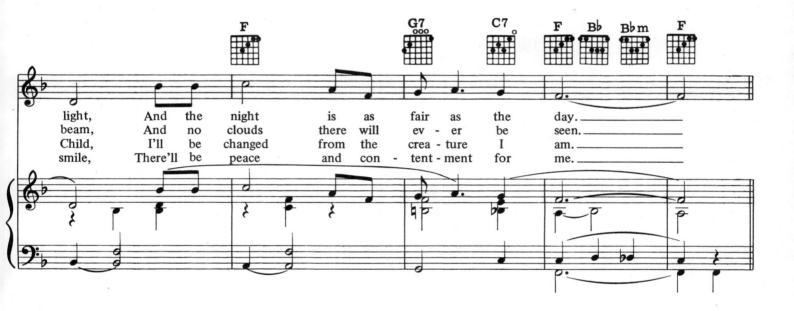

light, And the night is as fair as the day. _____
beam, And no night clouds is there will ev - er be seen. _____
Child, I'll be changed from the crea - ture I am. _____
smile, There'll be peace and con - tent - ment for me. _____

Chorus:

There'll be Peace In The Val - ley for me some - day, There'll be

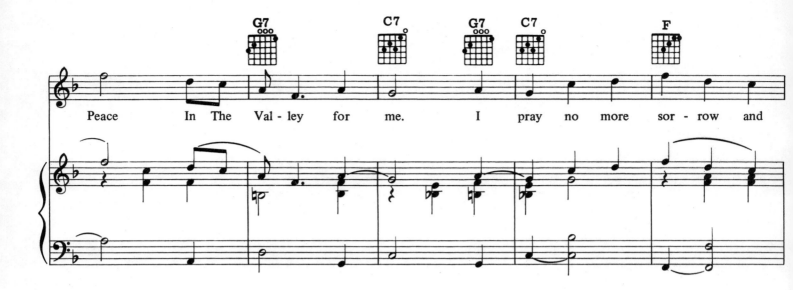

Peace In The Val - ley for me. I pray no more sor - row and

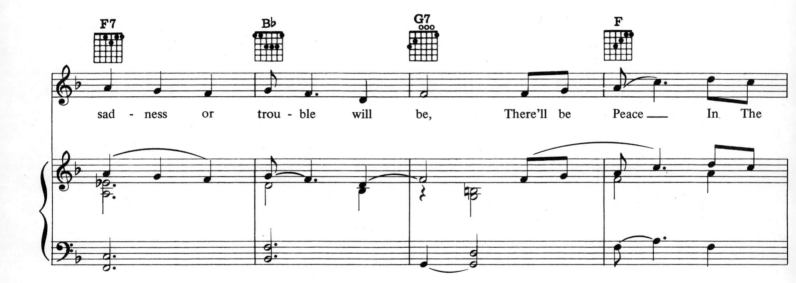

sad - ness or trou - ble will be, There'll be Peace ___ In The

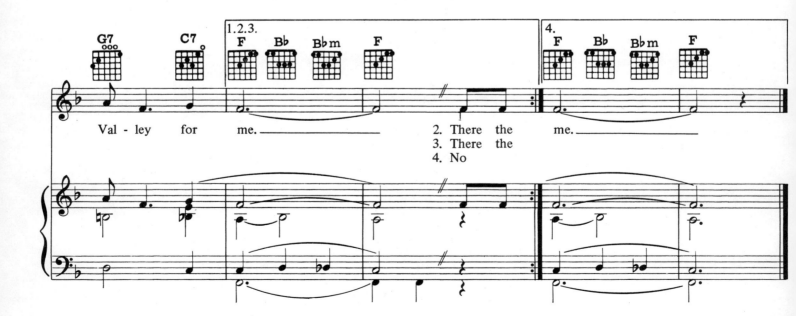

Val - ley for me. ___ 2. There the me. ___
3. There the
4. No

UNDERSTAND YOUR MAN

Words and music by Johnny Cash

Don't call my name out your win - dow, I'm leav - in',
give my oth - er suits to the Sal - va - tion Ar - my,

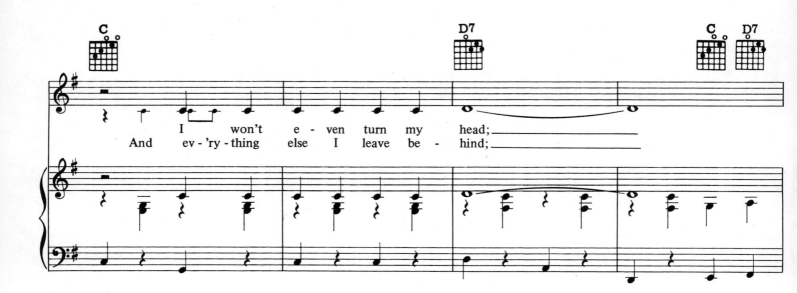

I won't e - ven turn my head;_____

And ev - 'ry - thing else I leave be - hind;_____

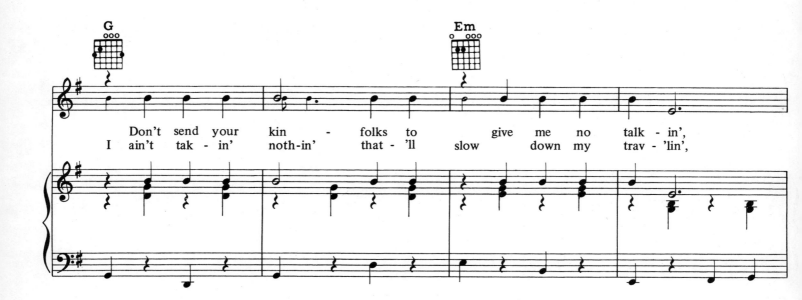

Don't send your kin - folks to give me no talk - in',

I ain't tak - in' noth - in' that - 'll slow down my trav - 'lin',

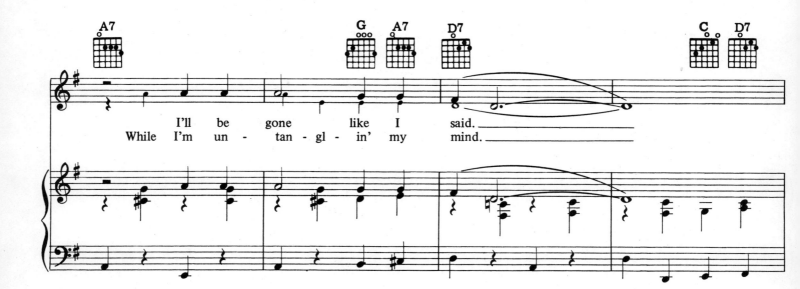

I'll be gone like I said._____

While I'm un - tan - gl - in' my mind._____

G7

You'd say the same old things that you been say-ing all a - long,
I ain't gon - na re - peat what I said an - y - more,

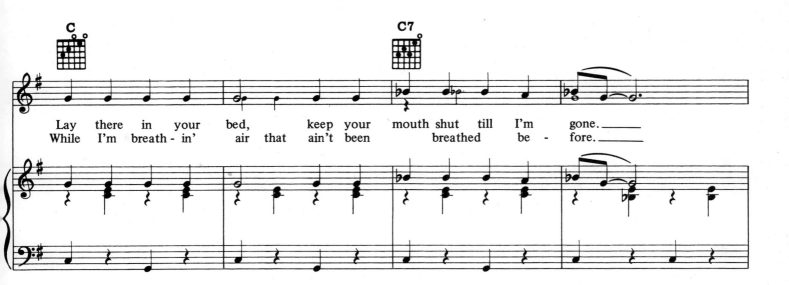

C   C7

Lay there in your bed, keep your mouth shut till I'm gone.____
While I'm breath-in' air that ain't been breathed be - fore.____

G   Em

Don't give me that old fa - mil - iar cry-in' cuss - in' moan,____
I'll be as gone as a wild goose in win - ter,

WABASH CANNON BALL

Words and music by A. P. Carter

1. From out the wide Pa - ci - fic To the broad At - lan - tic
2. Our east - ern states are dand - ies, So the West - ern peo - ple
3. She came down from Bir - ming - ham One cold De - cem - ber
4. Just lis - ten to the jin - gle And the rum - ble and the
5. Here's to old man dad - dy Clax - ton, May his name for - ev - er

shore She climbs high moun - tains Up - hill and by the
say. When she climbed Old Rock Is - land Took all her style a -
day. As she pulled in - to the sta - tion You could hear all the peo - ple
roar, As she glides a - long the wood - land To the hills and by the
stand; May it al - ways be re - mem - bered Through - out the

WALK ON BY

Words and music by Kendall Hayes

would-n't look so good to know some-one I'm not sup-posed to know.

Chorus:

Just Walk On By, Wait on the cor-ner, I love you, but we're

strang-ers when we meet. Just Walk On By, Wait on the

cor-ner, I love you, but we're strang-ers when we meet.

Fine

298

Verse 2:

In a dim - ly lit cor - ner in a place out - side of town, To - night we'll try to say good - bye a - gain, But I know it's not o - ver, I'll call to - mor - row night, I can't let you go, so why pre - tend.

D.S. al Fine

WALKING THE FLOOR OVER YOU

Words and music by Ernest Tubb

1. You left me and you went a - way,
2. (Now,) Dar - ling, you know I love you well,
3. (Now,) some - day you may be lone - some too,

You said that you'd be back in just a
Love you more than I can ev - er
Walk - ing the floor is good for

WELCOME TO MY WORLD

Words and music by Ray Winkler and John Hathcock

Wel-come To My World,_____ won't you come on in?_____

_____ Mir - a - cles I guess_____ still hap-pen now and then.

Step in-to my heart,_____ leave your cares be - hind,_____

Wel-come To My World_____ built with you in mind._____

Knock and the door__ will o - pen,_____ Seek and you will find,

Ask and you'll be giv - en,_____ The key to this world of

mine, _____ I'll be wait-ing here _____ with my arms un-

furled _____ Wait-ing just for you, _____ Wel-come To My

World. _____ Wel- come To My World. _____

WHEN THE SNOW IS ON THE ROSES

Original German text by Ernst Bader; English lyric by Larry Kusik and Eddie Snyder; music by James Last

WINGS OF A DOVE

Words and music by Bob Ferguson

Moderately bright

Verse: Tacet

Eb

1. When trou - bles sur - round us, ___ When e - vils
2. (When No - ah had) drift - ed ___ On the flood man - y
3. (When Je - sus went) down ___ To the wa - ters that

Ab 4 fr.   Fm   Bb7

come, ___ The bod - y grows weak;
days, ___ He searched for land ___
day, ___ He was bap - tized ___

311

You Are My Sunshine

Words and music by Jimmie Davis and Charles Mitchell

taken_____ and I hung my head and cried:_____
oth - er_____ you'll re - gret it all and some day:_____
oth - er_____ you have shat - tered all my dreams:_____

Chorus:

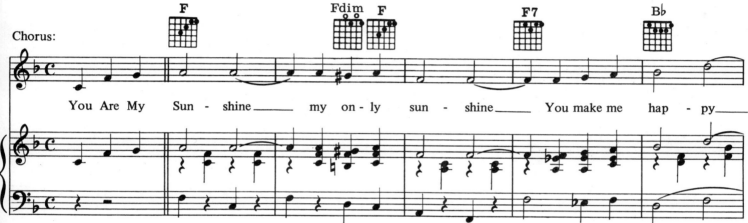

You Are My Sun - shine_____ my on - ly sun - shine_____ You make me hap - py_____

_____ when skies are gray_____ You'll nev - er know dear_____ how much I love you_____ Please don't

take my sun - shine a - way._____ 2. I'll al - ways way._____
3.You told me

rit.

YOU CAN HAVE HIM

Words and music by Bill Cook

Brightly

You Can Have Him, (her,) I don't want him, (her,) He did-n't love me (She)

an - y way. He on-ly want - ed some-one to (She)

play with, But all I want - ed was love to stay.

Verse:

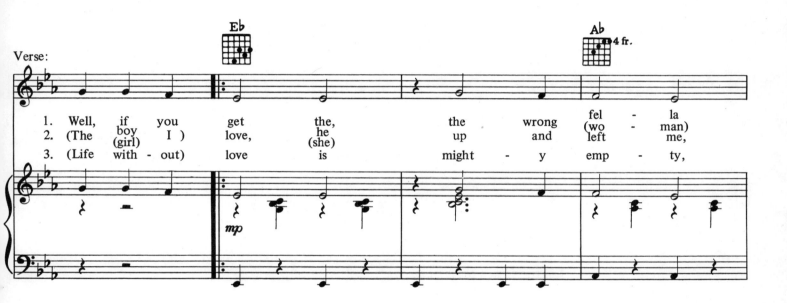

1. Well, if you get the, the wrong fel - la
2. (The boy I) (girl) love, he (she) up and left me, (wo - man)
3. (Life with - out) love is might - y emp - ty,

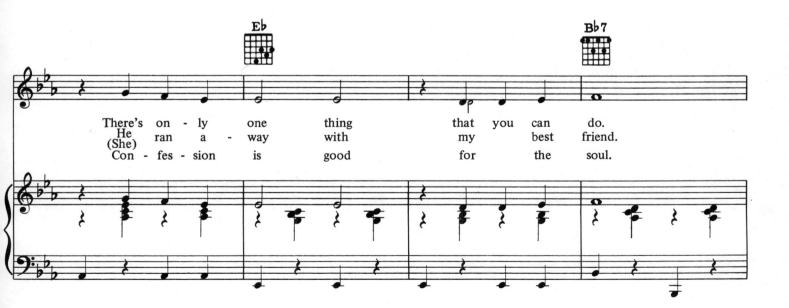

There's on - ly one thing that you can do.
He (She) ran a - way with my best friend.
Con - fes - sion is good for the soul.

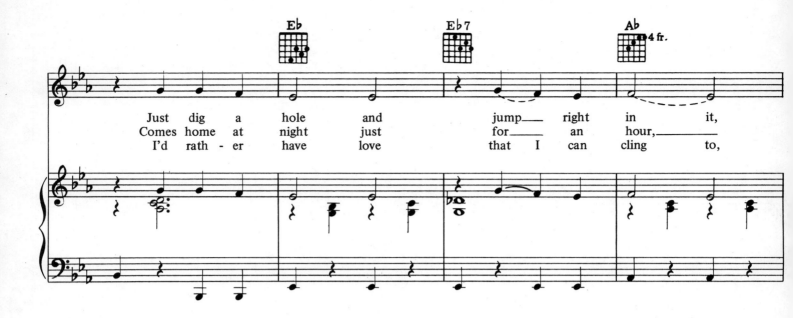

Just dig a hole and jump____ right in it,
Comes home at night and just for____ an hour,____
I'd rath - er have love that I can cling to,

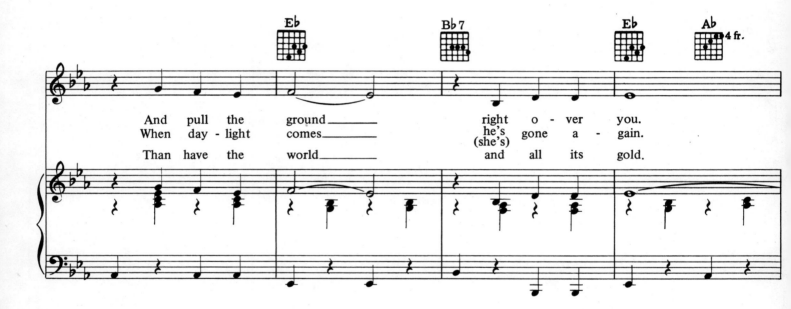

And pull the ground____ right o - ver you.
When day - light comes____ he's gone a - gain.
(she's)
Than have the world____ and all its gold.

Chorus:

Oh, You Can Have Him, I don't want him,
(her,) (her,)

He did-n't love me an-y way.
(She)

He on-ly want-ed some-one to play with,
(She)

But all I want-ed was love to

1.2. Eb   3. Eb

stay.   2. The boy I   stay._____
             (girl)
          3. Life with-out

YOUNG LOVE

Words and music by Carole Joyner and Ric Cartey

Moderately

They say for ev-'ry boy and girl there's just one love in this old world, And
Just one kiss from your sweet lips will tell me that your love is real, And

I ___ know ___ I've ___ found mine. ___
I ___ can feel ___ that it's true. ___

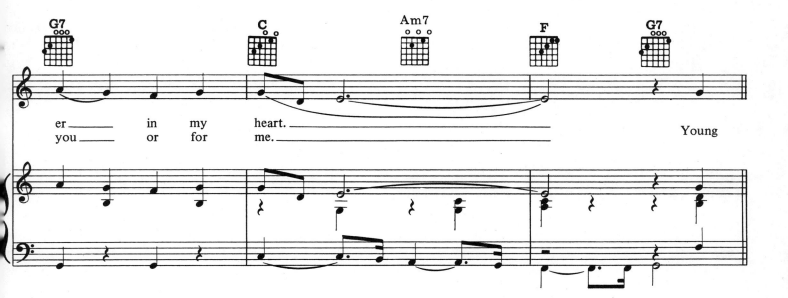

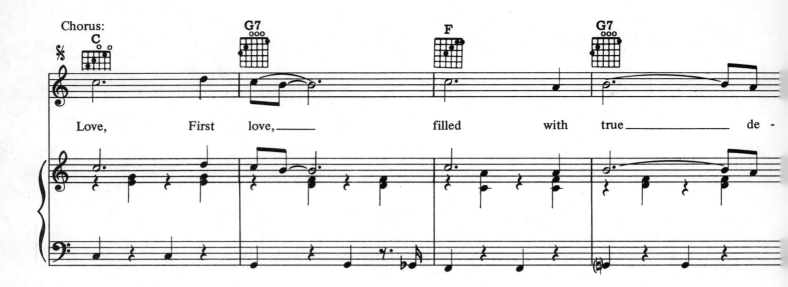

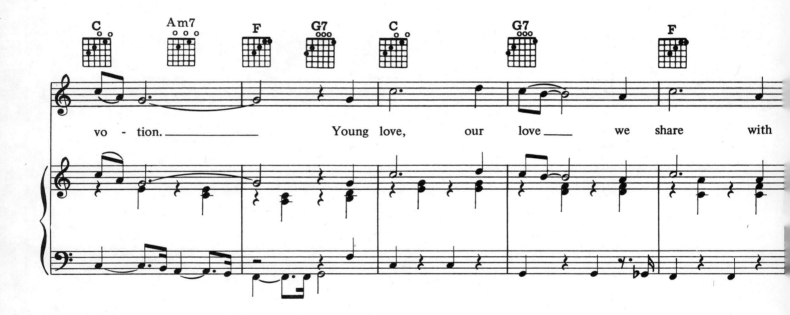

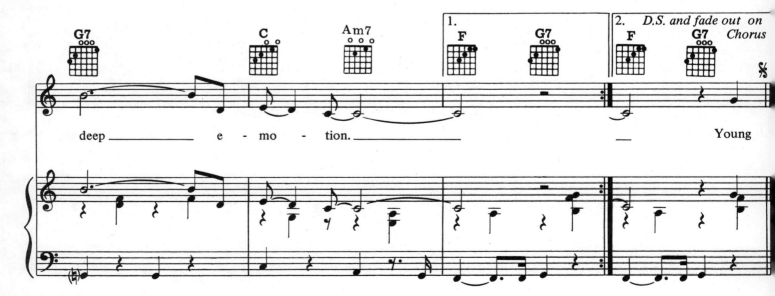